When her husband suddenly deserts her, Lora Ffennig is forced to abandon her simple, peaceful existence and work to support herself and her two young children, Rhys and Derith. But Lora's problems are only beginning . . .

The Living Sleep is the story of how one woman's courage and fortitude enable her to overcome the problems of enforced independence and, finally, to discover a more genuine happiness.

Also by Kate Roberts

FEET IN CHAINS

and published by Corgi Books

The Living Sleep

Kate Roberts

Translated from the original Welsh
by Wyn Griffith

CORGI BOOKS

THE LIVING SLEEP
A CORGI BOOK 0 552 11685 8

Originally published in Welsh
Translation to English first published by John Jones Cardiff Ltd.

PRINTING HISTORY
John Jones Cardiff edition published 1976
Corgi edition published 1981
Corgi edition reprinted 1986

This book is set in Century Schoolbook 10 on 11 pt.

Corgi Books are published by Transworld Publishers Ltd.,
61-63 Uxbridge Road, Ealing, London W5 5SA,
in Australia by Transworld Publishers (Aust.) Pty. Ltd.,
26 Harley Crescent, Condell Park, NSW 2200, and in New
Zealand by Transworld Publishers (N.Z.) Ltd., Cnr. Moselle
and Waipareira Avenues, Henderson, Auckland.

Made and printed in Great Britain by
Hunt Barnard Printing Ltd., Aylesbury, Bucks.

I

It was a bright Monday morning in May. Lora Ffennig went about her housework keeping as much as she could to the sunnier parts of the house, and these, in the long row of similar dwellings, were not numerous. Iolo, her husband, had gone away for the weekend; she had done the washing and ironing on Saturday so that she wouldn't have to bustle about when he came back tonight. Even after eleven years of married life she was still excited at the thought of his return. Not that it compared with her feelings when he came home from the army or the front. For then they were tainted with fear and anxiety.

Today things were different: his absence was merely a holiday from work, going to stay with a wartime friend, an Englishman from Shropshire. Strange, she thought as she went from the kitchen to the parlour to get tea ready for the schoolmistress who lodged with her, that he never spoke about this friend he stayed with, never answered her questions about him but changed the conversation. Not that it bothered her much, for she had never met him, and all she knew about him was that he was a farmer's son. But come to think of it, strange that he never gave Iolo some butter or bacon, scarce as they were, to bring home with him. Strange also that Iolo never spoke of inviting him here.

The afternoon sun reached the kitchen and brightened everything. The wallpaper was old, and to make the room in which they spent so much of their time look more cheerful, she had gone out in the morning

1

to buy a new rug, red and blue, larger than the old one, to put on the red-tiled floor, a great improvement. She had washed and ironed the curtains and the cushion covers on Saturday, put them all back, so that the room, with a clean white tablecloth, looked most attractive. She lit the fire in the kitchen and in Miss Lloyd's room, for it was still chilly. Lora wasn't one of those landladies who make sure that once spring cleaning was done, there would be no more smoke to soil the chimney until winter. She had been glad of Miss Lloyd's money as well as her company during the war, and was still glad now the prices of everything were going up. In the same mood of pride mixed with anticipation she had shown towards her kitchen, she put on a short-sleeved pale blue jumper and a pale grey skirt, her first time in short sleeves this spring. Middle age is creeping up on me, she thought, for I can't wear short sleeves in winter now. But when she looked at herself in the mirror, she didn't seem much older than when she married; more of a woman, perhaps, and less of a girl. Honey-coloured wavy hair, eyes a dark blue—almost as blue as a sailor's—and hardly a touch of colour in her clear skin. Slim and fairly tall, she moved effortlessly about her housework.

Derith and Rhys came home from school, and Lora gave them a drink of milk and a piece of cake in the back kitchen while waiting for their proper meal when their father returned between five and six. The beef for Sunday had been kept to make a stew for tonight, and there was enough fat rendered to make a rhubarb tart, all but ready.

The front door bell rang, and she went to open it, telling the children to stay in the back kitchen. She was astonished to see Mr Meurig, a solicitor and her husband's employer; she couldn't remember his ever having called here before.

"Can I have a word with you, Mrs Ffennig...just you alone?"

She took him to the front parlour.

2

"It isn't very good news I bring," he said awkwardly, as he sat down.

"Something happened to Iolo?"

"Yes, but not what you'd expect . . . nothing to be frightened about . . . he's alive and well."

"Thank goodness for that," she said, relieved.

"You were expecting him back tonight, and so was I tomorrow. But I got a letter from him by this afternoon's post, from London, saying he wasn't coming back at all."

"Why? Has he found another job, or what?"

"Quite possibly. But the plain truth is that he and my housekeeper have gone away together."

Lora could hardly take it in. It was all so unreal.

"Did *he* say this?"

"Yes. He asked me to tell you."

"I see," she said, without change of expression.

"Did you have any hint of this?"

"None at all."

"I can't say I was surprised myself. I found that whenever Mrs Amred went away, so did he. And every now and then someone hinted that they were friendly . . . well, you know how people are."

"I never thought there was anything between them."

Even if she'd ever doubted her husband, she would never admit it to a stranger like Mr Meurig.

"I'm very sorry," he said, rising. "Is there anything I can do for you?"

"No thanks . . . Anyway, I can hear Miss Lloyd coming now," she said hurriedly.

"But can't I do *anything*?"

"Well . . . I don't know who's going to tell his mother and sister. *I* don't want to break the news to them. Quite enough for me to try and tell Miss Lloyd or Mrs Roberts next door."

"I'll go with pleasure," he said. "Indeed it's my duty to do so."

"Will you really? That's very kind of you."

"Think nothing of it. I'll call again."

3

She went to the back kitchen, opened the door of the oven and finding all done, turned out the flame. The children had finished their snacks.

"Have we got time to go out to play before Daddy comes home?" asked Rhys.

"Yes," his mother answered. "He won't be back to-night. That's what Mr Meurig came to say just now."

"He isn't ill, is he?"

"No, he's all right, but something's kept him ...until tomorrow."

The two went out, but Rhys came back, hanging around the door and looking at his mother. But as he could see that she wasn't crying and didn't look upset, he felt sure that his father wasn't ill. All he noticed was that her face was redder than he had ever seen it.

She went to the other kitchen and sat by the fire, the brightness of the flames adding to the comfort of the room. Thinking it over, she decided that she ought to tell her neighbour. When Mrs Roberts saw her coming down the path towards her back door, she knew immediately that something was wrong. Normally Mrs Ffennig would just call out over the garden wall if she had something to say. She told her to come in and Lora gave her the news standing on the kitchen floor, as if she were repeating the Ten commandments.

"I'll come home with you now," said Mrs Roberts. "Some of the children will be here any minute."

She led her home and sat her down in her own kitchen.

"What can I do for you, Mrs Ffennig?"

"The greatest kindness you could do for me would be to keep people away, but I'm sure that's impossible. Would you be kind enough to tell Miss Lloyd, please? She's in the back parlour. And if you could give her her tea, some of the meat and the rhubarb tart."

Seeing Mrs Roberts passing through the kitchen with the golden crust of pastry, Lora succeeded in crying, and the next thing she knew was that there was a crowd in the kitchen, including her sister-in-law

4

Esta, and Esta was saying she would take the children home with her.

While they were all talking, Lora asked to be excused so that she could send word to her sister, and someone volunteered to post the letter. After all this was over, there wasn't much anybody could say. It wasn't as if someone had died. You could speak about a man to his widow, but not about a man who had left his wife. They all left except Mrs Roberts, who persuaded Lora to go to bed, promising to come in later. She climbed the stairs, undressed and went to bed like someone in a dream. Soon she heard the front door closing and Miss Lloyd going out.

II

Loti Owen sat in her parlour before a tiny grate, black and empty, with a white paper fan spread like a pair of wings across it. Her newspaper had fallen from her hand some time ago, and she stared at the grate just as she used to do in winter, seeing pictures in the glowing coals. Tonight she indulged in another delight, and that was of inventing ways of punishing people she disliked, and of these, her landlady was the chief at the moment. For her it was to be confined for a night in a refrigerator. For most landladies, the Easter holidays meant nothing more than blackleading the grate, but for Mrs Jones, it also meant making a white paper fan to put in the middle of it, the fan a farewell and a mourning card for the fire for the rest of the season. Loti could just imagine the zest with which Mrs Jones wielded the brush, the pout in her lips as she pleated

the fan, and then the look of satisfaction. She was quite
sure that at this very moment she was sitting comfortably in front of her kitchen fire roasting her legs,
reading her Sunday picture paper.

Loti looked at the table, waiting for it to be cleared,
the cheap thick crockery, and in the middle of the poor
tablecloth the bottle of sauce with nothing under it. It
would be cleared some time, she supposed, leaving the
white cloth and the crumbs and the bottle of sauce
there until the morning. How lucky her friend Annie
was to be with Mrs Ffennig, with a fire tonight, and
the table cleared ready for her when she came back
from school so that she could start working at once if
she wished to. And a good thing too, for people as innocent as Annie were not usually lucky in their lodgings, being born victims for rapacious landladies.

Thinking of Mrs Ffennig, her mind turned to the
husband. Where had he gone this weekend? There was
something wrong somewhere. She didn't like the look
of his books this morning in the office, and why had
that woman come in from the country to pay on her
house and not a word said about last quarter's? Could
it be that Iolo had ... but no, surely not. But there *was*
something the matter. He hadn't seemed interested in
his work lately, moving listlessly, as if his mind were
far away. What truth was there in the story about him
and Mr Meurig's housekeeper? There was plenty of
gossip about it. And this gave rein to another of her
hates, for Mrs Amred was one of those she disliked
without really knowing her. Her face was enough. Time
would show whether there was any truth in the story.
High time something happened in this sleepy little
town. And yet, everything seemed to be happening here
when she and Arthur were in love: then, neither the
cold sunless room nor cold-hearted landlady would
have mattered. Perhaps Annie might come in soon, or
she might go to her, for Annie would be sure to have
a fire. She got up to fetch her knitting just as the door
bell rang, and Mrs Jones brought Annie into the room.
Annie looked disturbed.

6

"Have you heard the news?" she asked after she had shut the door.

Loti put her finger to her lips and nodded towards the door.

"Sit down, and be careful."

Mrs Jones came in to clear the table.

"Don't say anything until I tell you to," said Loti as soon as Mrs Jones had gone out of the room. After she had finished clearing the table, down to the bottle of sauce and the cloth, Loti gave the signal.

"What's happened? Speak quietly."

"Oh dear," said Annie, almost choking. "Mr Ffennig has gone off with Mrs Amred." The only effect it had on Loti was that as she looked up from her knitting, the slight cast in her eye became a squint.

"When was this?"

"I don't know. All I know is that Mr Meurig had his lunch in town today and went home rather early."

"Yes, he had a headache."

"And with the afternoon post there came a letter from Mr Ffennig giving the news and asking him to tell Mrs Ffennig. This was before I came back from school. Mrs Roberts next door came to tell me and said Mrs Ffennig didn't want to see anybody much, but judging by the noise there were plenty of people in the kitchen."

"I'm sure there were."

"Why don't you say *something*? Aren't you shocked?"

"Yes and no. People have been gossiping about them for some time now. But I was just wondering..."

"What about?"

"Strangely enough I was thinking about them when you rang the bell."

"Oh!"

"I'd had a strange kind of day, thinking there was something wrong there."

"Did you know about the two of them?"

"No, it wasn't that...I don't know whether I ought to say anything."

"Don't if you don't want to."

7

That was enough to touch Loti's pride in her perception and ability to sense events before they happened, to put two and two together just like a novelist. Her anxiety to show this capacity overcame her prudence.

"Keep it to yourself, and whatever you do, not a word to Mrs Ffennig."

"I promise."

"As Ffennig was away today, I had to use some of his books, and a woman came in from the country to pay the mortgage interest on her house. I could see that she had missed three quarterly payments, but she said nothing about this. And when I asked her if she was paying what she was owing, she seemed surprised. No, she said, I don't owe anything but what I'm paying now. I was going to tell Mr Meurig about it, but I found he had gone home early."

"Lord help us! Poor Mrs Ffennig! I hope she never hears of it."

As if she were beginning to regret her indiscretion, Loti said, "Don't forget, it may only be a mistake. The record may be somewhere else."

"That's what a war does to a man."

"Don't you start on that note. The war is blamed for everything. If a man steals, it's all due to the war ... if he drinks or runs after women, it's just the same."

"Once you get a taste for travel, you get restless."

"Maybe, but it makes others fonder of their homes. But it does make people more shameless. Plenty of this kind of thing went on before, but people kept it quiet."

"All the more dishonest of them. But I can't make out what Mr Ffennig *saw* in that Mrs Amred."

"We don't know what a man sees in a woman. Not what you and I do, for sure. And he's got such a good home, too."

"Yes, but not many men marry for comfort. Except when they're old. There must be something about Mrs Amred to attract Iolo Ffennig."

"She's pretty enough, and that's about all I know, except that she's always cheerful. Save us from people who are always cheerful!" said Loti, knitting with more vigour, her eyes crossing.

"And there's the children," said Annie.

"Oh, they'll soon forget. All children are totally self-centred."

"I don't know what's come over you, Loti! How harsh you've become!"

"Look, Annie Lloyd, somebody must be harsh so that the rest can be reasonable. And I've always thought Mrs Ffennig a cold, remote sort of woman."

"She's not easy to get to know, I admit, but so much comes out once you get to know her better."

"That's true of all of us."

"I mean pleasanter things, and I couldn't hope for a better lodging."

"Oh, I can believe that she's full of principles and honesty and doing her very best in every way. And she's good to look at. But there isn't a spark of fire in her, and perhaps Iolo Ffennig would prefer less comfort and more excitement."

"He doesn't strike me that way."

"You can't tell, Annie. Neither you nor I are the type of woman with enough charm to draw husbands from their wives."

Staring at the grate, it crossed Annie's mind that Loti was trying to show how clever she was, and in doing so she was revealing much that was new of herself. Loti began to laugh.

"What's the matter?"

"I was thinking of his sister Esta. This will take her down a peg or two."

"She's sure to find a way of turning her brother into an angel and putting all the blame on someone else."

"That's the worst of belonging to a family of only two children."

Annie was thunderstruck. This kind of talk was going too far, and she might find herself saying something she'd regret, and suddenly it occurred to her that her friendship with Loti might come to an end.

"I think I'd better go," she said. "I must try to see

Mrs Ffennig before she goes to bed, much as I dislike it."

"Look," said Loti. "Do you think Mrs Ffennig might take me in to stay? She's got a spare bedroom now."

"Where?"

"She could take Derith to sleep with her and I could have Derith's room."

"I like the way you arrange other people's lives for them."

"She'll have to get money from somewhere."

"Her husband will have to pay towards her keep, and she can go back to the school if she wants to. If that happened, I'd have to leave."

"If she got a woman in to clean, she could do that and take us both in."

"I don't know about that. I must go now, anyway."

Loti lifted her head from her knitting and looked at Annie. Could it be that there was more in Annie than a kind, innocent girl?

Annie walked the pavements between Loti's lodgings and her own like someone trying to postpone penance, approaching the house as if it were a house of mourning. Indeed it would be easier if it were, for she knew what to say in such circumstances. Loti's talk had left a bad taste in her mouth. She had gone with the news expecting to find sympathy with Mrs Ffennig, but instead, silly suggestive and half-clever words. Loti was not a friend of Mr Ffennig, though you might have thought so tonight, either that or she wanted to find fault with Mrs Ffennig, and that touched a tender spot in Annie. When she had come straight from college to Aberentryd to teach, she had liked Loti and admired her, the way her talk differed from other people's, and she gave her total friendship, finding no fault in her. And she had shown her kindness and sympathy when the end came to Loti's love affair.

Tonight, however, she saw another side of her friend, heartless, mindless, harsh and suggestive, as if she were dealing with sums of money in the office rather than with people in trouble. Loti had become sour, too soon for one so young. Contradicting everything, too. She was astonished to hear her say a word in favour of Esta. She was glad she hadn't said anything more to Loti about Esta; it would have been so easy for her to tell how unhappy she was in school because Esta was always carrying tales to the headmistress as part of what she thought to be her duty as her secretary. As the school wasn't part of Mrs Ffennig's world there was no temptation to talk to her about her sister-in-law. It was to Loti that she unburdened herself of her greatest personal fears about school. Tonight something warned her against any further revelations. Why hadn't she taken the hint when Loti suggested sharing her lodgings? A while ago she would have welcomed it. Something gripped her, a chilly kind of irritation, small enough compared with what had happened where she lived, trivial in face of the tragedy that had overtaken Mrs Ffennig. And yet her instincts told her that the two were related, although she couldn't explain why, as if she had dropped a ball of wool in her lodgings and dragged the thread with her to her friend's house.

Before going in she saw someone standing in front of Aleth Meurig's house, the furthest house on the left of the road, a little spot of light by his side. It was the solicitor himself, sure enough, in something of a fix tonight, his clerk having run away with his housekeeper. As he opened his gate, the light became a circle as he swung it round. She waved her hand and went in.

All was quiet and dark. She looked into the kitchen, the fire out, the rug turned back. Going upstairs and reaching the landing, she heard Mrs Ffennig calling her from the bedroom.

"Come in, Miss Lloyd, and forgive me for calling you."

She was in bed, her face a feverish red.

"I came to bed, tired out with all the talk in the kitchen, and it was getting so hot there."

"I'm very sorry," said Annie falteringly. "I didn't like to come to the kitchen before going out, seeing so many

11

people there. There's nothing I can say except that I'm sorry."

"What is there to say? I can't say much myself, I'm so upset. I had no warning at all."

"Don't try to talk if you don't feel like it. Would you like a cup of tea? Won't take me a minute to make one."

"Oh well," said Lora hesitatingly, and then eagerly: "Thanks, and bring one for yourself." And then, as Annie went down to the kitchen, she felt that there was one spot of light in the darkness, but doubted whether she had any right to that much. She enjoyed her tea and the bread and butter.

"Don't go," she said to Annie. "I can't sleep, and if you don't mind, it would do me good to talk."

"By all means, if you'll feel better for it."

"You can't make a parade of your troubles, and as everybody was trying to talk at once I couldn't say anything. My sister Jane is coming here tomorrow. I sent word to her, but she's too close for me to talk to really. Can you follow me?"

"Indeed I can. I keep everything back from my family."

"Forgive me for asking, but did you know there was anything between Iolo and this woman?"

"I saw nothing myself, but people were talking."

"That kind of talk would never reach me if I didn't go looking for it, and there was no need for me to look for anything. We were happy enough together as a family, and Mrs Amred was always in and out of the house."

Too much so, Annie thought to herself.

"You must remember," Lora went on, as if talking relieved the pressure of her thoughts, "Mr Meurig didn't know much of her history when he engaged her. A man in his position has to take anyone he can get these days, without taking up a reference."

"True enough. Not like it used to be."

"To tell you the truth, I didn't think much of her one way or another. There are some people who make you

12

think that everything they say comes out of a jug filled with paper, and you know there's nothing inside. She was always cheerful, always saying the same kind of thing, but I don't think she ever gave any thought to what she was saying."

"You'd better go to sleep. I'll be up in the morning to give you and the children breakfast."

"Esta has taken the children home with her. I couldn't object with all those people there. Thanks very much all the same."

In bed, all the events of the evening revolved in Annie's mind. The night before all had been quiet, a new week beginning like so many before. Dislike of school on Monday morning, as on every Sunday night for weeks and months. Tonight something else beside Iolo leaving his wife had happened, she herself felt uncertain of even beginning to know people. Loti, instead of being her ideal, was now merely someone to be criticised. And Mrs Ffennig was no longer merely a landlady, but someone in whom she could confide.

She felt sorry for her, but could never plumb the depths of her tragedy. It was bound to be as isolated as a stook in the middle of a hayfield, and her own problems like wisps of hay at the edges. One of them was probably having to find new lodgings. Two things only had made her content to stay in Aberentryd: Loti's friendship and her comfortable lodgings.

In the next bedroom Lora Ffennig was wide awake, her mind revolving round one thing, turning and returning to it like the blade of a butter churn, one thing only, that her husband had left her, unable to see a step into the future or to think of the change that would come over her life. She couldn't even think of the children, nor of Iolo as an individual, to try to find why it had happened and whose fault it was. She was like a blind person struck in the head, not knowing who had thrown a stone at her and why, unaware of where it came from, conscious only of her pain. Exhausted, she fell asleep, and the last image in her mind was of her sister-in-law Esta, sitting by the kitchen door in the

13

afternoon, scowling like an angry child, finding the talk of the neighbours who had called to sympathise so hateful that she had got up suddenly and said that she would take the children home with her. Lora would have liked to say no, but she didn't. She was more conscious of Esta's dictatorial ways than of anything the others had said.

Aleth Meurig stood in front of his house, leaning on the gate. Sad and angry though he was, there was an element of the humorous in the situation. His clerk and his housekeeper both gone, no-one to look after the house, short of staff in the office. At any rate he was free to breathe in his own house, even if he had to cook and wash up, and the impact of another personality had been lifted. He hadn't had a moment's kindness since his wife died, except the pretence of it from Mrs Amred for a few weeks until she found that there was no hope of her becoming the second Mrs Meurig.

The patrons of the Red Lion had the right rude word for one of her kind with a brightness in her eyes that was no reflection of what passed through her mind. She was too mean to put more coal, his own coal, on his own fire, or to give him the food he paid for. Her eyes on him all the time he was in, watching how he ate the poor food she gave him, waiting for his reaction to what she ordered from the shops. Little did Iolo Ffennig know her, nor what was in store for him. They must have been head over heels in love.

He couldn't say that he liked Ffennig. He was difficult, able enough in a way, given to repeating what other people said and that with an air of originality. He had noticed for some time that his knowledge was confined to newspaper headlines. He ought to have gone on and taken the examinations, but he hadn't. Not from laziness, for he could work when he liked. Lack of ambition, perhaps . . . not entirely, but a certain dumbness, determined to do what he wanted, but not what other people wanted. Content to stay as he was because that differed not only from what others expected but also from what they did. Wishing to differ

14

and half opposed, without showing this except by silence, withdrawing into himself. He had never seen him in a temper: how much better that would be than the inexplicable mood of his when he was shown some other way of doing something. He wondered how his wife handled him when he didn't want to do something but wouldn't say so. It would take someone very clever to know him and handle him. Well, the storm had broken. He was sure that Mrs Ffennig knew nothing about what had gone on under her very nose. He thought of his own Elizabeth, who had died when their love was young and passionate and exciting, and how hard it was to be deprived of this.

He looked at the houses in front of him, most of them with lights in the parlour like moonlight through the mist, their curtains closely drawn; behind each one there were secrets the world knew nothing about. Innocent enough in some, doubtless; anxiety about health or money, afraid that the children wouldn't win scholarships to the grammar school ... that was true of some of them. Others quarrelling, some afraid of saying anything that might give rise to a quarrel and so keeping their feelings under control. Someone laden with a feeling of guilt to which he couldn't give expression. There had been one such outburst in Iolo Ffennig's house, after long brewing. For that matter, something might be on the point of breaking out in other houses. In some, it would fester instead of breaking out.

The light went on in his former clerk's bedroom and he saw Mrs Ffennig drawing the curtains, and before the last was drawn he caught a glimpse of her face and that swan-like neck of hers. No wonder some thought her the prettiest woman in the town. What a waste of beauty in a town like Aberentryd! She ought to be in Paris or London, dressed to match her beauty, mixing in the best society. She probably hadn't much to say even in her own language, for she had no opportunity to talk with men and women of intelligence. Perhaps the conversation he read in novels was little better than that he heard between Loti and the other clerks,

15

and that it was the art of the novelist that made it seem better.

Even if Mrs Ffennig had the means to buy better clothes, when would she have a chance to wear them in this grey and ordinary town? In chapel on Sunday, and then run home to change so as not to spoil them when cooking. On market day when meeting all the folk from the countryside. On prize day once a year in school. Women like Lora Ffennig were content from wedding day to the grave with nothing more than a week's holiday in summer. But why dream other people's dreams for them? That was exactly the way he himself had lived. Working to hasten the end of the day. But at one time Elizabeth was waiting for him. Since then, nothing.

He heard footsteps on the pavement some distance away and turning in to Mrs Ffennig's house. It was Annie Lloyd, back from her visiting. He raised his hand to her, not knowing whether she saw him. A kind gentle country girl teaching the town children instead of being with the cows and calves. She would have looked well in a cotton bonnet, and he could imagine her handling a hay-rake with her back swaying. He thought he'd better go in and go to bed. He felt unhappy, but his mind turned towards the woman across the road. He could not hope to fathom her mind. Tomorrow, the townspeople would be all agog, sinners seeking whom to blame, the saints in their joy, all athirst for news. And the lies that would be going the rounds!

III

The two children rushed into the house about ten in the morning, and Rhys fell on his knees on the arm-chair, his face buried in its back, his little body bowed, crying his heart out. Derith stood by the corner of the table, half-smiling shyly.

"Come, come," said his mother. "Things will get better soon, don't break your heart."

She sat in her chair opposite him, and the sight of him deepened the pain in her heart.

"We must all cheer up and be brave. Perhaps Daddy will come back again."

Derith ran to her mother, sat on her knee and buried her head in her bosom. Rhys turned towards his mother and said boldly, "It isn't because Daddy has run away that I'm crying."

"Then why?"

"I didn't want to go with Grannie and Aunt Esta last night. I wanted to stay with you. I didn't sleep a wink."

"Nor did I."

"And so it would have been better if we'd both been awake together."

"Aunt Esta thought it would be less work for me."

"I don't want to go there again."

"Why do you say such a thing?"

"Because I want to be with you."

"There's no reason why you shouldn't be with me and go to see your aunt and your grandmother."

"Things are different now." He put his head on her shoulder and began crying again. "Mam, I don't like Aunt Esta."

17

"Don't you?"

"That's why I don't want to go there again."

"Has she done anything to you?"

"Not to me, but she and Grannie was muttering things about you last night."

"Muttering? You don't know what you're saying."

"Yes I do ... talking quietly between your lips."

"I know too," said Derith, raising her head and looking at her mother's face for the first time since she came in.

"You don't know anything of the kind. Don't listen to her, Mam. She went to sleep as soon as she got there."

"No wonder," said Lora, "bewildered with all those people."

"And Aunt Esta said that Daddy wouldn't have gone away but for you," said Rhys.

"Oh!"

"That you thought more about us and the house than about him."

"Indeed. Did you say anything?"

"Not at first. Then I said, 'Look, it was Mrs Amred who made Daddy run off with her, not Mam.' That's right, isn't it?"

"Yes dear."

"Tell me why he wanted to go off with her and not with you?"

"I don't know."

"Because he liked her better than you?"

"For a while, perhaps. But you're too young to understand things like that, dear."

"Indeed I'm not, the boys are always talking in the school yard—"

"About what?"

"I don't like telling you. They've been teasing me for a long time, saying that soon I'd have two mothers, and worse things than that."

"What? No, no, don't tell me."

"Nothing bad, just saying that Daddy would soon

18

have two wives, and I couldn't make out what they meant."

"Why didn't you tell your mother?"

"It puzzled me, for I knew that you were my mother and that you'd never let Mrs Amred come here to live. And I thought you'd be even more puzzled, but that you'd understand some of it and that would worry you."

"Didn't this puzzle worry you?"

"Yes, but I tried to forget it."

"And failed, I'm sure."

"I didn't like those eyes of hers, always looking at you."

He began to cry again, and now Derith joined him. Lora drew their heads together and put her chin upon them. And that was how they were when Lora's sister Jane walked into the kitchen. The three of them quickly recovered themselves.

"Could we have something to eat now?" said Rhys. "I'm starving. I couldn't eat anything at Grannie's."

"I'll get dinner ready now," said Lora, motioning to her sister to keep quiet.

Today, eating the cold meat, she didn't feel the blow as much as yesterday. Her sister's presence was a help, and they understood each other well enough to be able to enjoy that meal at any rate.

The children went to school in the afternoon, and Lora could tell the way Rhys hung back that he hated the prospect of facing the other children. She decided to write to the headmaster asking him to make things as easy as possible for Rhys. Not that there was any need to write, but she knew that the fact that Rhys had the letter in his hand would help him to face the children that afternoon.

"Well now," said Jane, after the children had gone, "what's happened?"

"Only what I told you in my letter."

"So it's really true?" said Jane, as countryfolk always ask about bad news.

"This isn't something to pretend about."

"How was I to know that there hadn't been some misunderstanding?"

"It's perfectly true. Iolo wrote himself to Mr Meurig and asked him to come here to tell me."

"The scoundrel! And she's even worse."

"I'm not going to say anything about it now. I might be sorry later on."

"You're not going to take that scoundrel back?"

"What's the good of using bad words about each other?"

"Well then, what are you going to do?"

"What do you mean?"

"For money."

Jane, like many others not involved in tragedy, jumped ahead and left the sufferer in suspense.

"Dear Jane," said Lora, "I haven't thought of that yet. I haven't had time to take in what has happened, nor really to believe it."

"You've said yourself that he's gone, and you might as well begin to think now as later about how you are going to live. But can't they make him pay towards your keep and the children's?"

"Who are they?"

"I don't know who does such things ... the law, I'd think."

"The law can do nothing unless I ask, and I'm not going to have my name dragged through the courts here."

"Anyone would think it was you who had gone off."

"That's the way we've been brought up."

"I wonder where that woman was brought up?"

"Mrs Amred? God knows. Mr Meurig didn't know much about her when he engaged her."

"And what will the poor man do? He lost a very fine wife, I'm told." And then, as if the idea had suddenly struck her, "Why don't you go and housekeep for him, or have him here as a lodger?"

"I'm ashamed of you, Jane! Just think what people would say, that Iolo had reason enough for going off, and how Esta and her mother would gloat."

"I don't know what put it in my mind. Just that I'm an innocent countrywoman."

"I wish the world were as innocent."

"I don't see why you should bother about Esta or her mother. They don't matter to you any more, nor can they say you've done anything wrong. But I know what you're thinking, that it would delight Esta to find some-one else in the wrong."

Lora felt that she couldn't continue the discussion with her sister. There was nothing more to say. She began to clear the table.

"How is Owen?" she asked.

"Middling."

The way she said it shocked Lora.

"Always coughing and looking ill," said Jane, with a frown.

"Has he seen the doctor?"

"Yes, he has to have an X-ray."

For a moment Lora forgot her own troubles.

"Does he eat properly?"

"Only in the evening."

"That old quarry is no place for a man like him."

The whole of the past history of her family ran before her eyes like a film, the damage done to it by the quarry, leaving only her sister and herself.

Suddenly she was overcome by a feeling that had struck her often during her married life. How often she had taken comfort in the thought of her family! Had all the happiness of wedded life made up for the loss of the family? She felt sure that if she could have a real heart-to-heart talk with Jane, she could say the same about her life with Owen. What if it really were tu-berculosis, the quarryman's enemy, that Owen had? She was fond of her brother-in-law.

As her sister went off, Lora promised to come to Bryn Terfyn to see them soon, but Jane said Owen would be sure to come to see her first.

Carrying on with her housework in the afternoon, Lora felt that it had been thoughtless of her to have let the children go to school that day. Remembering

21

what Rhys had said about the boys' remarks, she could imagine how cruel they would be today. Derith and her class were too young for it. But as for Rhys...

That moment Esta came in, holding Derith by the hand, with just the same kind of face as the night before, stubborn, sulky and grieved. A gap had sprung up between them, of which Lora thought she was the more conscious. Rhys came in and went straight past his aunt into the back kitchen.

"Hello," said Esta, but Rhys didn't answer.

"Can Derith come home with me for a while?"

"Can I, Mam?"

"Well...do you want to?"

"Yes," she replied, hopping on one foot.

"Would you like to come, Rhys?"

"No thanks, Aunt Esta."

"Mother's in bed," said Esta.

"What's the matter with her?" This was the first time she had thought of her mother-in-law.

"This business was an awful shock to her."

"So it was to us all."

"But you must remember that she's his mother."

"Look Esta, this kind of talk does no-one any good. I've got two children and I've got to find some way of providing for them."

"Some people can stand up to something like this better than others, and mother was always tender-hearted."

"I've got to try to face the world, and neither you nor anyone else knows what I feel inside. It would do none of us any harm to be a bit more cheerful."

Esta began to cry.

"I never thought my brother would do such a thing," she said. "I thought the world of him."

"So did we all. And he may come back," said Lora without conviction.

"Even if he does, he'll have brought disgrace on our family."

"There are worse things a man can do than running away with a woman who isn't his wife," said Lora. "And

22

there are others in this town who'd like to do the same if they dared."

"I'm surprised you take it so lightly."

"I don't. I was trying to see it from Iolo's point of view. He must have been fond of this Mrs Amred for a while, anyway. It would be much worse if he'd stolen money. Of course that kind of thing can be hushed up. What you are objecting to is the publicity."

"I'm still surprised you can take it like this."

"I'm neither taking it nor rejecting it, but trying to look sensibly at it. I don't know whether you'd like me to go about as if I'd driven Iolo from home. You forget he went of his own free will."

"I think I'll go now," said Esta. "Come along, Derith . . . I'll bring her back." This time Esta left looking more sorry than sulky.

"I hope your mother gets better," said Lora dryly, over her shoulder.

She sat by the fire, thinking, turning over everything in her mind, sorry now for what she had said to Esta. But soon she was indignant, remembering how all her concern had been about herself and her mother, without a word of sympathy for her brother's wife. Rhys came from the back kitchen and sat by her side.

"Don't worry, Mam. Never mind Aunt Esta and Grannie."

"Why didn't you tell me Grannie was in bed?"

"I never thought . . . she's always in bed."

"Tell me, Rhys, how were things in school today?"

"Just the same."

"Did the boys say anything to you?"

"Say what?"

"You know how children are. Did they tease you?"

"Nobody did. No-one said anything in class, and Dafydd was trying to keep me away from the other boys in the yard in playtime."

"Good for him. Now listen to me. This trouble will end some time, and then the boys may begin to tease you and to say nasty things and to provoke you. Try your best not to listen to them. If you take notice of

23

them, they'll provoke you all the more. But if you turn a deaf ear, they'll soon be tired of it all."

"I'll try my very best, but perhaps I can't. Are you worrying, Mam?"

"Yes, bach. But we must all try not to, so that we can be happy again."

"Derith doesn't seem to mind, does she?"

"No, she's too young. She doesn't remember much about your father before he went to the war."

"Daddy wasn't the same to me as he used to be when he came back from the war."

"Wasn't he?"

"No. He didn't want to talk much to me, nor to play with me as he used to."

"True, but then he'd been away from us for so long."

"And become a little shy, perhaps, just as I was when I went back to school after being ill at home long ago."

"Maybe. But don't worry too much. You'd better go out to play with the boys while I get tea for Miss Lloyd and for us all."

"I'm not keen on going. I'd rather stay in the house with you."

"Just for quarter of an hour."

Rhys went out, unwillingly.

After tea, Mr Jones the minister called. She couldn't say she was glad to see him on this occasion. In the troubles that usually came the way of his flock, his sympathy was that of a minister rather than that of a friend. But this was an uncommon happening, and it was hard to find words of comfort to give her.

"I'm sorry about what has happened and that I couldn't come here yesterday. I've had to sympathise in all kinds of troubles in my time, but never in one like this."

Lora had nothing to say to him.

"I don't know what would be the best thing to wish for for anyone," he stumbled on.

"Hoping they could be sensible, I'd say."

"Are things as bad as that?"

"Every shock is."

24

"I *am* sorry. I daresay many have told you to be brave, for the children's sake."

"No-one said anything else yesterday."

"There's a lot of truth even in such trite sayings, you know."

"Yes, unfortunately. But when you hear them time and again, you begin to wonder whether the blow has fallen on the children or on you."

"True enough. It would be much better if I were wise enough to do as the old folk used to and say, 'I hope she is strong enough to bear the blow'."

Lora felt better able to talk.

"That's what I've been saying to myself since yesterday."

"People are strange, you know. From the pulpit I can say to them, 'throw your burdens on the Lord', but I find it hard to do that in talking to you like this."

"Yes, it is, for when you are in the pulpit you're not face to face with people in trouble, and it's easy enough to say such things to a congregation, some of them with no troubles, others with plenty, but you don't know which is which. But when you meet someone and try to say something to comfort them it's very hard, isn't it?"

"Very. There's such a gap between you."

"There is, and it's very difficult to get close to anybody. There's a gap between you and people you love, sometimes."

The minister was silent in his turn. But then he said, "Mr Ffennig was a pleasant chap."

"Yes."

"But we don't know how people are made up. There are some things in the nature of some of us that go back a long way, and then burst out in a flood where you'd least expect. I hope you can forgive him."

"I don't see how forgiveness has anything to do with it. When you forgive someone for something, it elevates you above him, though you are no better than he is."

"Let me put it another way. I hope you are not angry with him, for after all he has sinned, you know."

25

"Do you know, Mr Jones, that by now I haven't any idea what sin is." He looked surprised. "Things are different when they happen in your own house."

"I shouldn't have spoken in this way to you, Mrs Ffennig, but it was you who lifted the curtain off your mind a bit. I came here to ask how you were. Can I help you in any way? To be blunt, my dear, have you enough money?"

"Thank you Mr Jones, but I haven't got round to such things yet, and I don't know how I stand."

"Will you tell me if there's anything you want? Come and tell me."

"Thanks very much, I will." The gap between them had narrowed.

Derith came home and went to bed. Rhys insisted on staying up to keep his mother company and to have a cup of tea with her. Just as they were finishing the front door bell rang.

"There's no end to people calling," said Rhys. "Perhaps it is someone for Miss Lloyd."

But it was Mr Meurig who came into the kitchen.

"I'm sorry to break in on your meal ... don't stop."

"We were just finishing. Rhys is going to bed."

"I'll go now Mam, since you've got company."

After he had gone, his mother said, "He wants to be with me all the time, as if he were afraid of my being alone. This has hit him very hard."

"I'm sorry."

"Won't you have some supper, Mr Meurig?"

"Don't trouble yourself about me ... you've had yours."

"It won't take a minute. Miss Lloyd doesn't have much because she has a substantial meal when she comes home from school."

"It's wrong of me, but I can't refuse. I've had no decent food for days nor indeed for some years."

"Oh, was that the kind of woman Mrs Amred was?"

"Much worse than that. But I don't know whether you want to talk about it."

Somehow, Lora felt drawn nearer to this man she

hardly knew than to anyone. She had never taken much notice of him before. He was tall, somewhat bowed, a high forehead under thick black hair. She had never been close enough to him to see kindness in the deep-set blue eyes, never having thought of them but as the shrewd eyes of a solicitor.

"Do go on," she said. "It will do me good to talk to someone who knew them both fairly well."

"Well, if you'll forgive me for saying so, she was a bitch was Mrs Amred, of no use to me. But that's how they are nowadays. A bitch in other ways, too. She did all she could to get me to marry her. No need to go into details."

"Good gracious!"

"I'm telling you this to try to hearten you, for you can be sure she used the same tricks to take your husband away from you."

"Iolo must have been weak."

"Yes, in a way. He was unsettled."

"That I can believe."

"I'm sure lots of people must have told you since yesterday that the war was to blame for it."

"They did."

"In my opinion, it wasn't the war itself that did the damage, but the chance it gave for travel. That's what makes men crave for a change from sitting in an office all day."

"That and living in a dull little town like this."

"Yes, an old town that has lost for years now what it had by way of culture."

"But after all, running away with another woman is something more than a wish to travel."

"It is. There are people who can't live the whole of their lives with their first choice of mate. They get fed up. No interest in anything else. I try to comfort myself, having lost Elizabeth, that it was before life together had made familiarity a burden to us."

"Possibly. But I can imagine what you call familiarity turning into a ripened conserving that makes middle age and old age a pleasant time of life."

"You may be right," he said, staring into the fire.

Why was she talking like this to this man? she asked herself. Was it because he had suffered, or because he knew Iolo better than others did? Or because he spoke so nicely about his wife? They began to talk about something else.

"Would you like to take over your husband's job in the office?"

Lora was startled.

"Thank you, but it's all too sudden, not having taken time to think at all about my future. And as I'm used to teaching, it might be best for me to go back to school."

"Yes. I never thought of that." As he went out he left five pounds on the table and had gone before she could thank him.

Lora was tired, and she was glad that Miss Lloyd only stood at the kitchen door to say goodnight and to hope that she slept well.

But sleep wouldn't come. The talk with Mr Meurig had excited her curiosity, as if she had lifted the corner of the plaster on a cut and it had begun to curl and she longed to carry on until the whole of the plaster was off.

Tired as she was, she wasn't really anxious to see what lay beneath, but the act of removing the plaster pleased her, like working out a sum or taking off a scab.

That weakness of which Mr Meurig spoke . . . she had never noticed it in Iolo. She had never thought of him as weak or strong. Their life had been too quiet to call for a display of strength or weakness. The children had given no trouble. Come to think of it, her husband hadn't taken all that much notice of the children, and Rhys had been more aware of that than she had, at least after he had come home from the war. Before then, he had doted upon Derith, who was then only two, but when he came back that was all over, just as a child tires of a toy. The thought of his attitude towards the children brought something totally different into her mind, the memory of something buried for

28

years. When they were courting Iolo told her a lie, and for weeks it festered in her mind. Only when they were together could she rid herself of it, and as soon as they parted, back it came to trouble her. One night it worried her so much that she decided to give him up and cease to regard him as someone she could spend her life with. But the idea hurt her so much that her mind moved the other way, and she managed to persuade herself that she hadn't heard the lie, and that if he never lied to her again she would forget all about it. So well did she succeed in this that the memory of it disappeared, and as she had never found him lying again it ceased to worry her. Tonight she remembered the lie, remembered him saying it, but not what it was. She tried to recollect, but failed. Again and again she searched in her mind, this way and that, but without success. Exhausted, she fell asleep.

IV

Loti was sick of sitting staring at the empty grate and decided to go to see her friend Annie. After what she called the catastrophe she felt a little shy of going, because she was afraid of meeting Mrs Ffennig. Although she knew her well enough as Annie's landlady, she had now become a different being, as if she had lost a limb. When the bell rang, Mrs Ffennig came to the door, the two children holding her hands. Loti couldn't say any more than "How are you tonight? Can I please see Miss Lloyd?"

She rushed into her friend's room, sat down, and for some time kept silent.

"What's the matter with you?" asked Annie.

"Oh dear," she replied, "I've been so stupid. I just couldn't say anything to Mrs Ffennig just now. I'm sure she thinks I blame her just because Ffennig works with me and that I'm on his side."

"No, I don't think so."

"In fact I felt too sorry for her and couldn't say anything to her, and I'm afraid there's worse to come."

"Is that true?"

"Yes, unfortunately. Ffennig hadn't entered in the books the money paid by the woman from the country. And I had to tell Mr Meurig."

"Of course."

"If I'd had money I'd have paid it myself, for Mrs Ffennig's sake, not for his, the wretch."

"Is it much?"

"No, not really. But, you see, there might be more."

"What a pity!"

"I felt like a murderer, looking at Mrs Ffennig and the children. It's dreadful to see someone who doesn't know the worst that's ahead of them, when you do." Loti was nearly crying.

"Would you like me to tell Mrs Ffennig that you were upset about some other matter before you came, that you couldn't tell her, and that you were enquiring how she was?"

"Would you really?"

Mrs Ffennig came in with Annie and Loti was able to explain to her without showing that she was concealing anything. And she apologised for not having come to her at once after what had happened.

"Don't worry," said Lora. "I'll be glad to see you again when everybody's forgotten."

"Thanks very much."

That moment the front door bell rang and they heard Rhys and Derith racing to the door and crying out "Uncle Owen," and taking someone to the kitchen.

"Forgive me," said Lora. "I'm sure it's my brother-in-law."

Lora found Owen much changed since she last saw him, face and hair a uniform grey.

"I'm very sorry, dear Lora," he said.

"Look, Owen," she replied. "We won't talk about what's uppermost in our minds now. So many people have called here recently that I'm almost deafened with talk about sin and trouble and war and children." She winked at Owen and turned her eyes towards the children.

"Here," he said. "Could you go to the shop and get some cigarettes for me and some sweets for yourselves? Here you are."

"Just a minute," said Lora. "I want Rhys's help just to take a cup of tea to a young woman who's called to see Miss Lloyd. Something had upset her before coming in. And we'll have a cup later."

"But I had a meal before starting. I came early from the quarry so as to catch the bus."

"Never mind, you can do with another. I've been lucky enough to get a piece of pork to boil. Get me the tray, Rhys."

Soon the tray was ready for the two women in the parlour, with bread and butter and cold pork, and the same for Owen in the kitchen.

"What a treat!" said Loti when she saw the tray. "That old creature in my place is worse than ever. She won't even cook me a little fish when I come back from the office. This is really good."

"Eat away. I had a good meal when I came from school."

"Mrs Jones has never forgiven me for throwing the bottle of sauce out of the window."

"*What* was that?"

"Well, the night you came I felt so fed up looking at that sauce bottle standing there on the table like a monument that I aimed for the dustbin outside and hit it with the bottle."

"Weren't you afraid she'd kill you?"

"Not a bit of it. She knows she won't get anyone else, and she knows that it would be hard for me to find another lodging because my holidays are so much shorter than those of teachers. Did you get a chance of a word with Mrs Ffennig?"

"About what?"

"About my coming here."

Annie knew the question would come. "No, I don't like asking so soon. She hasn't had a chance to pull herself together yet."

"No, poor soul, nor does she know all there is to know. And that Esta," Loti went on. "Just *stalks* about the school. She stopped me in the corridor today, and do you know what she said?"

"No, I don't."

"'How is she?' she asks. 'Who?' says I. 'Lora,' she says. 'She's bearing up wonderfully after such a blow,' says I. 'Oh,' she says spitefully, 'she'll make a proper martyr of herself.' And off she goes before I could answer her. Pity she doesn't know how dishonest her brother was, but Mr Meurig won't say anything. I'm sorry for him, too."

"Yes, but losing a wife through death is nothing compared to this."

"True," Loti replied, staring at the fire.

Annie regretted that the conversation had taken this turn, but Loti didn't pursue it any further that night.

"It's the coughing at night," said Owen as he ate his bread and butter.

"You'll get some satisfaction after you've had the X-ray."

"Yes, either that or my sentence of death."

"Don't talk like that," said Lora. "You forget that it's wonderful what they can do nowadays to cure people."

"I know that. But you can't live without money. And what would Jane do while I was having treatment?"

"We've all got to suffer such things and try to live," said Lora.

The moment she had said that, she regretted it. The marks of suffering were already to be seen on him, not only suffering but also hard work, a life of working ever since he was fourteen.

A frank handsome face, his hair greying most attractively. So far as looks went, he might have been a

Minister of the Crown, but the slate had hardened and coarsened his hands, the dust had affected his breathing and deformed his shoulders.

"Strange, isn't it, Lora, that so much of our suffering is caused by someone else."

"And much of it by ourselves."

"Yes, but I was thinking of the quarry owners. If in the past they had thought about the workmen, they would have found some way of conquering the dust. But profit came first. And look at you, now, it isn't your fault that you are in this mess."

"My fault was to marry Iolo." This again without premeditation.

"Yes, but then you couldn't have known that this kind of thing would happen."

"No, I wasn't clever enough. Either that or I was blind. I'm sure that this, or something like it, must have been characteristic of him from the start, only I hadn't seen it."

"My dear Lora! We never see faults when we are in love. Think of that great chapter of St Paul's."

"We've both heard it read often enough when there was nothing to trouble us. It's always to other people that trouble comes. How could I sit in chapel tonight and listen to 'Charity never faileth' after this misfortune coming my way? St Paul might have put it all into three words: Love is blind."

"But think of the loss to the literature of the world."

"Maybe," said Lora bitterly. "It seems to me that a lot of it is written about half-truths. We enjoy listening to that chapter, but somehow it doesn't work when you have to face up to life."

Owen burst out laughing until a spasm of coughing broke out.

"Forgive me," he said. "I can't help laughing at the idea of you and me discussing St Paul on a week-night."

"Yes, it is rather funny. His standards were so high. When we do the same someone deflates us and all comes tumbling down."

"You're getting bitter, Lora, something I couldn't

imagine. You've always had something to live for. Do you remember how you were always afraid of something happening to your father and mother?"

Lora couldn't see the connection.

"You lived for their happiness, and you were delighted when your dream came true and they had their own house after the children had grown up. And that was thanks to you."

"It all came to nothing."

"Yes, they had worked so hard beforehand that their health gave way."

"But life is strange, isn't it, Owen? To think that poverty drove them to their end while they were comparatively young. It was that that they suffered from. And we are little better able to stand other trials."

"There you go again, expecting too much from the morrow, always. I'm sure your father and mother were happy enough bringing you up, even in poverty. They were able to enjoy the little things that came their way while we look for luxuries."

"True," Lora said thoughtfully, "There are worse things than poverty."

"Than their kind of poverty. They struggled against their surroundings. They never went without food, like people in China who are always starving."

But Lora couldn't turn her mind to the people of China nor anywhere else. Her mind kept turning back to her own troubles.

The children came back and it was time for the bus; the three of them went to see him off. A clear sky as good as a bottle of medicine to Lora, and as bitter, strange and remarkable. To be out was to enter another world now.

"Goodbye Uncle," said the children. Their voices mingled with the sound of the bus as Lora tried to say, "I hope you'll get good news about your health."

"When can we go to Bryn Terfyn, Mam?"

"We'll go quite soon. There's light enough now after school."

"And stay out late?"

"Yes, but you ought to be in bed by now, Derith."

Lora noticed that their interest had changed somewhat, though Rhys wasn't very pleased at being sent to bed after supper.

Annie Lloyd came into the kitchen to say goodnight.

"Loti was very grateful to you for the meal you gave her," she said. "It was a real treat for her. She's very unhappy in her lodgings. Mrs Jones won't cook anything for her, and this week things are worse than ever. Loti threw the bottle of sauce out of the window in a fit of temper."

Lora laughed.

"She isn't really wild, but every now and then she gets fed up, and she was sick of seeing that bottle of sauce left on the table all day, and all night for all I know."

"A thing like that would sicken me too."

"And now she's begun to think that no-one would take her as a lodger because she gets such short holidays."

"She hasn't got a home, has she?"

"No, and as her sweetheart let her down she hasn't got a hope of having a home of her own."

"It's hard for her."

"It is, and she's a bit odd at times, like when she threw the bottle of sauce out of the window. And she can be a bit prickly, too. She didn't use to be."

"That's a pity."

"I don't really mean prickly. But whatever you say she takes the opposite view just to be different, although you know very well that she agrees with you."

"How bitter she must be!"

"That's what I keep on trying to tell her. She's young enough to catch another fish."

"She may be one of those women who can't bear to think of another man when they've been crossed in love, just because it meant so much to her."

"Even so, she ought to pull herself together. She's got brains enough to pass exams and get a better job, or at least to find some other interest in life. Lucky for

35

her it all happened before they got married."

Annie realised at once that she had put both feet into it but Lora, seeing her confusion, said diplomatically, "You can't tell. Things are always different, and all we know is what goes on inside ourselves." Reflectively she went on, "I wonder if Miss Owen would like to come here to stay, if you were willing to share the parlour with her. I'll have a spare bedroom now." Lora gave a sigh, and Annie blushed, feeling that she had in an underhand way asked for this favour while dwelling on her friend's misfortunes.

"She'd jump at it!"

"And you wouldn't mind?"

Annie hesitated a moment. "Of course not."

"I *could* let her have the front parlour, but if I have to go out to work it would be easier and cheaper for me to light only one fire. I'll have to get someone to help me with the house."

"Naturally. Can I tell Loti?"

"Of course. I'm sure I can put up with her, and the two of you are friends. Much better than taking in a stranger."

I wonder, Annie said to herself.

V

A fine Friday morning, and to all who were tired of winter, the first morning of summer. Lora had to go shopping, and the sooner she went out to face the world the better. Life in the kitchen with so many people coming in had become unbearable. Whether or not she wanted to, she would have to meet the townsfolk, and she felt the time had come for her to go, even if they turned their backs on her. For even this, like everything else, would soon be forgotten. She would have liked to wear one of last summer's frocks, but contented herself with an old grey coat and skirt and a blue blouse. At present, thanks to Mr Meurig's gift, she had the usual amount of money to spend. She would have to call at the Education Office and the bank some time.

The sun's brightness spread everywhere, reflecting back from the cars, the surface of the street and from the windows, tar melting like treacle and catching a woman's heel. Shop windows seemed full, the greengrocer's full inside and out, women having to draw their skirts to get near the counter. Colours of flowers and fruit, cars and bicycles, children and dogs, everybody cheerful and greeting one another in the warmth of this first day of summer. Lora passed through them without any attempt to look at them, greeting only those who spoke to her. Some came up to her as if nothing had happened, others suddenly turned to examine a shop window, giving the impression that they were looking closely at something they had spotted before they saw her, completely absorbed until she had passed them. A few stood in groups talking, stopping when they saw her and then whispering when she had gone.

Some middle-aged women, expensively dressed, sat at a cafe window, smoking cigarettes over their empty coffee cups, idly dropping the ash into the ashtray, smoke hanging like grey nylon stockings in a shop window. They turned their heads like birds in a cage, looking casually through the smoke at passers-by as if they were of no interest, some looking up from no other reason than that someone had passed between them and the sun.

The minister crossed the road towards her but said nothing except, "I'm glad you're brave enough to venture out," and left as if afraid that Lora remembered the end of their conversation in her house.

She saw Esta coming out of the bank and crossed the street to meet her, but all that happened was that

Esta said, "I'm in a great hurry, just taking in the savings bank money, and Miss Immanuel has a lot for me to do the moment I get back."

Lora stood still, thinking of all she had done for that girl. The headmistress was her God now that she was sure of her job, but she had smarmed her way with so many people, including Lora, before she had got it. Lora crossed over to the grocer's who greeted her warmly, shook her by the hand and offered her a chair.

"Just come in here for a minute," he said as he opened the door of the counter for her to enter the parlour behind the shop.

"Well, Mrs Ffennig," he said when they were inside, "would you like to run an account until things are better?"

She was touched and murmured her thanks. "It's kind of you, but I'm all right for this week. But later on if you were so kind, when I've decided what to do, I'd be very grateful."

"As long as you like . . . your name is good as gold here, and everywhere else so far as I can make out."

His wife came in with coffee and biscuits on a tray.

"Just a bite to keep you going in this heat. I'm glad to see you coming out. At a time like this, the less said the better."

Lora's eyes brightened, and she showed her gratitude in her enjoyment of the coffee.

Leaving the shop, she walked towards the Education Office, but hesitated about entering. Bureaucracy in every window, and she couldn't imagine herself facing all the clerks and the head himself. She realised that it was in this part of the town that Mr Meurig's office was, and it was hard to imagine that Iolo wasn't there somewhere. She turned back, lacking courage to enter. She walked towards the bank, but was afraid to go in. Little wonder—she never liked finding out how much she had, it was always less than she thought because she forgot the bills she had paid. She went home as she had done a hundred times before when she had to hurry to get Iolo's dinner ready by twenty to one. No need to hurry today, no dinner to prepare. Ambling aimlessly towards the house she felt widowed: hitherto there had been the vacuum of expectation; now, no-one to expect.

Before she could indulge in any more self pity, she saw someone in black standing by the door, head bowed, tall, thin as a pencil. She realised it was her Uncle Edward, dressed as he was at the beginning of the century, tight black trousers, long black coat buttoned high, bowler hat on his head, an old-fashioned high collar and dickie, the latter bursting out of his waistcoat. Her mother's brother: she rarely thought of him, for he would have little to do with her after her marriage. When she was young she got an occasional shilling or half-crown, once or twice a pound when she was in college. But no wedding present, and he never came to see her.

"Where have you come from?" she asked.

"From home, and from my troubles. How are you?"

"Bearing up, but that's about all. But we won't talk about it now. We'll have a bite to eat first."

She fried some Spam, an egg and some potatoes.

Over the meal, Edward Thomas tackled her.

"Where's your husband gone?"

"How should I know?"

"Taken a woman with him, hasn't he?"

"So they say."

"Hasn't that woman across the road gone?"

"Yes, it looks as if they've gone together."

That was the only way to talk to the old man. No use asking him how he knew: she knew him too well.

"The old scamp!" he went on. "And she's no better. She must have been hard put to it to find a man if she had to steal another woman's."

"Now don't start condemning people. After all, he's still my husband."

"You don't mean to tell me that you still think anything of him?"

"I said nothing of the kind. What do you know about things like this? You never married, never fell in love. And yet you're just the same as other folk wanting everybody to think you once did."

He laughed as he said, "Yes, like that old maid up the hill still looking for a husband until she was eighty, lifting her skirt to show her white petticoat on the way to chapel, still rubbing her cheeks with a bit of red paper from round a packet of tea."

"Poor soul!" said Lora. "A sad story."

"Sadder still if she'd caught someone. Pity people don't find out more about the family they're marrying into before getting married. I never thought much of Iolo's family when they lived near me."

"I don't suppose they thought much of you either."

"They were all so hoity-toity, and as for that girl Esta, she behaved as if the sun rose from her bottom. She even put on gloves to go for a walk up the mountain."

"That was pure ignorance."

"She'd never play with other children except to play school, bossing everybody and even caning them. I'm sure some of their ancestors were slave-owners in Jamaica."

"Don't be so silly!"

"She just had to boss everybody, and neither she nor Iolo ever told the truth."

"Children rarely do. How they'd enjoy calling you an old miser hoarding all his money!"

"Nothing dishonest in that."

"No-one can make money honestly."

"Why are you so cantankerous? You used to be such a nice girl once. I don't know what comes over you people who get a bit of education and go and live in a town. You've come to talk just like a preacher."

"If living in the country makes people like you, then give me the town."

But nothing Lora could say would ever get under his skin, tough as the hide of his mountain ponies.

"I've come here to make you an offer," he went on. "Would you and the children like to come up to look after me? I wouldn't charge any rent, but you'd have to find your own food and I couldn't pay you anything."

"Heavens above! What do you think I am?"

"I knew it. Too much of a lady."

"Just think a moment. You're behind the times, you and your clothes. How do you think I clothe and educate the children?"

"Schooling doesn't cost anything nowadays, and I'm sure you've got clothes enough to last your lifetime."

"True enough, if I were like you. But the children, what about them?"

"They could help, and I'm sure you've got money tucked away somewhere after keeping lodgers so long."

Lora sighed and gave it up as a bad job. He was hopeless.

"There isn't much I can do now," he said. "The rheumatics."

"You're quite lame, I noticed."

"There isn't much to do up yonder, and it's a good house."

"I'm afraid we could never live together without quarrelling."

"Why should we quarrel?"

"I don't know, except that all who share a house do. Don't you ever think how lucky you are to be living alone?"

"I've never tried living with anybody."

"No, and it's too late now. Why don't you get a woman in to clean the place?"

"They charge so much."

"How long do you think you're going to live, and what are you going to do with your money?" Too delicate a question for him to answer.

"I could manage pretty well except for washing clothes," he said.

"Surely one of your neighbours would do that for you!"

"I don't want everybody seeing what I wear."

"Would you like me to wash them for you?"

"Could you? " he asked hopefully.

"If you'll send them down and collect them. They could come on the bus." Instead of thanking her, Ed-

41

ward Thomas laughed half-heartedly, and Lora didn't know whether it arose from conceit or from the joy of finding another fool ready to work for nothing.

She took him to the bus, and the difficulty he had in climbing into it affected her strangely. An object of pity to anyone unaware of his circumstances, but he had no compunction about entering his bank. A topsy-turvy world, but nothing would induce her to change places with him. She kept looking at him sitting there, not even turning his head towards her, perhaps unable to do so, just staring ahead, his walrus moustache touching the window, his hat down over his eyes. She walked forward for another sight of him, but he didn't see her, and off he went staring straight ahead like a man sitting in chapel.

She didn't feel like doing anything when she got home. The dishes were still on the table, everything so little to her liking that she sat in the armchair, remembering this day week, the last day she saw Iolo, busy putting a clean shirt, socks and collars on the bed, even putting out his cuff links. She could see the open suitcase on the bedroom floor, four clean hankerchiefs in one corner, clean collars in another, another pair of socks and his slippers. Hot with anger, she got up suddenly and set to work furiously. Soon the children would be back from school and Miss Lloyd would want her tea, and then she determined to have a quiet restful evening.

When Mr Meurig called that night, she didn't want to see him or anybody else. She was tired of all this talking, talking in a void, everybody thinking of himself and not commiserating with her. No-one could understand her feelings, nor could she reveal them to anyone. The irony of it was that the one person she could unburden herself to was the very cause of her desire to do so.

Mr Meurig made no attempt to stay—he was in a hurry, he said, having heard of a reliable woman to come in every day, leaving him only his supper to prepare. He had come to bring Iolo's pay for two weeks,

42

and when she demurred explained that Iolo was entitled to a fortnight's holiday anyway, and to the pay
unless he returned before the fortnight was up. Before
she could thank him properly, he had hurried out.

Peace in the house, the children out playing, Miss
Lloyd having had her tea and gone to the parlour. She
went to fetch the tea things so that she could sit quietly
in the kitchen, calling Derith in to go to bed. She looked
at the envelope Mr Meurig had left on the corner of the
table, half afraid to open it, oddly enough remembering
a friend who received such bad news in a letter that
ever afterwards she left them unopened for days. And
she herself felt that inside everything closed there was
something evil.

Eventually she opened the letter and found in it
more money in one sum than she had ever seen since
she married. Of course, it was a fortnight's pay. Slowly
she began to work things out, dividing it in two and
deducting Iolo's pocket money, only to find there was
something wrong. She tried again, but it wouldn't come
out right. Perhaps Mr Meurig had given something
extra. But that wasn't likely, for then he would have
made it up to a round sum instead of these pounds
shillings and pence. She remembered how she had felt
in bed the other night after he had called him a weakling; it was as if she had just begun to pull the plaster
off a cut, determined to go on doing it to find out the
very worst. Had Iolo kept more money for himself than
he said he did? He didn't spend much on himself, only
on cigarettes, and he wasn't a heavy smoker. And some
sweets for the children occasionally. She continued to
doubt, remembering what her uncle had said this
morning, that Iolo and his sister were given to lying.
That lie Iolo had told her before their marriage—she
couldn't remember what it was.

The children ran in, Derith in tears.

"What's the matter?" she asked.

"She wants to come with me to Dafydd, to see his
rabbit hutch," said Rhys.

"You wouldn't care for it, dear."

43

"But I want to go with Rhys."

"I'll tell you what," said Lora. "We'll all go to the pictures tomorrow."

"Can Dafydd come?" asked Rhys.

"Of course he can."

"I'll go and tell him now...I won't stay and then I can be here with you."

"You stay with Dafydd a bit while I put Derith to bed."

"I don't want to go to bed," said Derith.

"It's so light you can stay up a bit."

Derith began to cry.

"You let Rhys go everywhere," she said.

"He's bigger than you."

"I can walk as well as he can."

"Rabbits are dirty things anyway, and you can have some chocolate after your milk."

Derith stopped crying and finished the chocolate.

"Are we really going to the pictures tomorrow?"

"Of course we are."

"You promised once before but we didn't go."

"Well, we're going tomorrow, and Dafydd with us, and then we'll have a nice supper afterwards. Come and get washed and go to bed."

Lora stayed by Derith's bedside in the attic...she didn't know why. Half asleep, Derith said, "If Daddy was with us we'd fill the whole row, wouldn't we?"

"Yes," said Lora. Derith fell fast asleep.

When Rhys came in, he found his mother staring at the fire. "Are you tired?" he asked.

"A bit."

"Dafydd's father has made him a fine rabbit hutch, plenty of room for them. It isn't right to keep them in small boxes, is it?"

"No."

"I'd like to keep rabbits."

"You'd get tired of it. They're a nuisance when you go away."

"But we never do."

"No, unfortunately. But you'd have to look out for

44

dogs and cats, and you'd be heart-broken if they died, wouldn't you?"

"Yes, I would.".

"Supper now. I'm going to bed early tonight."

Miss Lloyd came in and seeing Lora looking so exhausted, went up and brought down a sleeping tablet. And that night, Lora slept the whole night through.

VI

Lora rose at six in the morning, wide awake, the doubts that had troubled her the night before so remote and unreal now that they did not hurt so much. She started work with a new vigour, so different from the previous days when the house had had little more than a wipe and a rub. Miss Lloyd was away for the day and wouldn't want dinner, so she'd make a simple meal for herself and the children. She raced through her work, trying to rid her mind of her doubts, only to find other troubles taking their place. Last night the children had complained that they never went away anywhere, and it was true. Derith was right in saying that she had once broken her promise to take them to the pictures, and so was Rhys when he said they never went away. She tried to justify herself: money was scarce, but there was also that relic of the hardness of her own upbringing still active within her ... "I wasn't allowed to go at your age." But there were no such things as pictures where she was brought up, and the weekday chapel meetings satisfied them all because they knew of nothing better. And there she was, applying the standards of her own childhood to her own children for their good, forgetting that children want what other children have.

How hard it was to understand a child, to know what interested them and what was best for them! Derith's last words before going to sleep made her wonder how much the child really longed for her father. By now, Lora was looking forward to going to the pictures if that would comfort the children. Hundreds of them, unending noise, a blend of thunder and rustling, smell of sweat, dirt, soap, hair oil, and Lora in the thick of all this racket able to forget everything except her immediate surroundings in the dark of another world for half the afternoon. To come out into the open air was to return to the world of pain.

"What did you like best?" Rhys asked her at teatime.

"The birds' nests and the chicks and the food going down their necks."

"It nearly made me sick to see the food in a lump," said Dafydd. "Made you think it would come through the skin."

"Yes, their necks are long," said Lora.

"And ugly," said Rhys.

"They're not very pretty at that age."

"Not like young rabbits," said Dafydd.

"What I liked was the horses going hell-for-leather," said Derith."

"Where did you hear that?"

"It's what the boys beside me said."

"You're not to say it again, remember."

"Why?"

"It's not nice."

"Why?"

"Because it's ugly. You're not to say it."

What Lora really felt was that the boys had the power to describe what they saw, and correctly, as the horses came forward in the film. Why must we pretend? Would the children be any the worse for using slang? Were the slum children any the worse?

Going out to play, Rhys asked could Dafydd come to supper—he'd go and get fish and chips for everybody, to save trouble, but Lora said she had some fish and would make chips, and Dafydd could come. She had to get a meal for Miss Lloyd coming by the eight o'clock train and it would be no more trouble to prepare it for them all. She was glad to find Dafydd taking Rhys's mind away from what had been bothering the boy for days.

When Miss Lloyd came in, she insisted on eating with them in the kitchen.

"We've been to the pictures," Derith told her.

"What did you see?"

"Horses going..." she looked shyly and smiling at her mother, "like I don't know what." Then she laughed triumphantly with a "there that's tricked you" look and went on, "and there were tiny chicks being fed, their necks as long as Auntie Jane's goose." She stretched her neck as far as she could. "That's how they were, and their father and mother fed them, the father going far away to fetch food and the mother putting it in their beaks and it went down their necks. We could see it going."

"Who told you all this?"

"The boys by my side, and they used bad words."

"Miss Lloyd doesn't want to hear them," said Lora.

Clearly, Miss Lloyd didn't want to hear any more about anything, for she got up and said she was going to bed early.

Lora had hoped that she would sit by the fire with her after the children had gone to bed...she didn't know why, except to talk about anything on earth, just to prevent her mind dwelling on the doubts that troubled her last night. Somehow, the day had brought her a little comfort, like a sudden burst of sunshine on a dull day.

In bed she tossed and turned and couldn't sleep, and by now what relief the day had brought had disappeared and doubt came rushing forward like the figures on the screen. It would be so much better if there were someone she could confide in. It was only with her friend Linor Ellis, in London, she could be perfectly frank. But she couldn't convey her doubts in a letter, for they were merely suspicions. She had told her that

47

Iolo had left her, but that was just plain fact. To write about her suspicions, or even to refer to them, was to risk giving a wrong impression. If she told Owen or Miss Lloyd, she knew they would not betray her confidences, but how would they react? What if they changed their minds and blamed her? Hadn't this always troubled her, this fear that those she liked would do so? Wasn't that why she was disappointed with Iolo? In the end, wasn't it herself she was sorry for? Or did she want to defend herself in some way by letting them know, so that someone else should know in case anything happened to her? She decided to keep to herself her suspicions about Iolo's money—not only that but also to dismiss them from her mind. After all, he might have had things to pay for out of his salary that she knew nothing about.

VII

Lora let a whole week go by without going to the bank or to the director of education, indulging in a state of reverie from which she had no wish to emerge in case fresh doubts should arise. She did her housework, but without zest. As she got Loti's bedroom ready for next week she tried to forget why she was doing it, and that it was once her own room. She looked upon it as a room in which murder had been committed, and did not mind someone else having it.

On Monday of the second week there was a letter from the director asking her to call at his office as soon as possible. She wondered why, unless perhaps Mr Meurig had spoken to him. It was washing day and she made that an excuse for not going then. Tomorrow would do. She had to earn money somehow, merely to survive.

She found him very kind, without trace of official-dom in his manner, making her feel quite at home, giving the impression that she was doing him a favour rather than the other way round, and asking her to start work with the girls in Derith's school. Admiration in his glance as he offered her a chair, and in the tone of voice when he said she would like the school. It made her think of a mother reassuring her child on its first day. So many years had passed since anyone had shown such concern for her that she wondered whether he was not mistaking her for someone else. She had not thought that men like this could possibly exist. Her spirits rose and she entered the bank to ask for her passbook. It was in a thick and imposing envelope, but she was not tempted to open it on the way home. She put it on the dresser while she prepared her dinner and decided to open it later. It looked as if it had been there for days. As she was now alone for the midday meal she didn't bother much about cooking, and throughout the previous week she had looked forward to this hour because it would give her a chance to rest and think before getting tea ready for Miss Lloyd and the children.

So today, after warming up some stew and fruit, she sat in the armchair, and later got up to fetch the pass-book. She opened the envelope carefully and began to examine the entries in the book. She felt the blood draining from her face and nearly fainted. The book fell on the floor. Recovering herself, she realised what had happened. Iolo had taken £40 out of their joint account the day before he went away, leaving only a couple of pounds there. She felt as she did when, a mere child, the pendulum of the grandfather clock fell down in the kitchen in the middle of the night; not knowing what had happened, thinking Judgement Day had come, rushing to her mother's bed in terror.

She jumped out of her chair and without even put-ting on her hat went straight to Mr Meurig's office. If

Iolo had stolen her money he might first have taken someone else's, his employer's.

The office was quite near, and she could think of nothing else until she knocked at the door. She stammered a request to see Mr Meurig, was taken into his room, and he dryly asked her to sit down. Then he relaxed somewhat and said, "Something has upset you, Mrs Ffennig."

"Yes, I want you to tell me whether Iolo has taken any of your money."

This was so unexpected a question that he hesitated before replying.

"Money? What money?"

"It's true," she said.

"What is true?" he asked, more confidently.

"That Iolo has taken money from the office."

"Who told you that?"

"Nobody, just instinct. He's stolen my money."

"That doesn't mean he's taken money from here."

"I don't believe it," she said, her eyes flashing.

"Try to calm yourself, Mrs Ffennig," he said coolly. For a moment he thought that Loti Owen had been talking to her friend who had then told Mrs Ffennig, but dismissed the idea.

"There'll be no peace for me until I know the whole truth. I've just come from the bank and I found that Iolo has taken £40 out of our joint account, and it was my own money, and I felt sure he'd have tried to take someone else's before taking mine."

"Had you any reason to suspect, before today?"

She had calmed down somewhat, but was on the verge of tears. "Yes," she said quietly. "I saw there was something wrong when you brought me his pay, that he was keeping more of it for himself than he ever told me."

"I see."

"I wasn't absolutely sure, though ... I thought there might have been other things he had to pay for. But I'm certain now."

He said nothing, looking down at his fingernails, so

50

she went on, "Mr Meurig, will you please tell me, was there anything wrong with his money matters here? My mind would be more at ease knowing than doubting."

He pondered for a moment as she looked at him more closely, as if a new thought had suddenly come into her mind.

"Mr Meurig, you surely don't think someone in this office has been telling tales and that they reached my ears?"

"Not at all. You wouldn't have come here as you did if that had happened. I could see that something had really upset you."

"That's how it was, only twenty minutes ago I opened the passbook, and the other idea only struck me on the way here. May I explain?" —

"Yes, but wait a minute." He rang the bell on his desk and asked the girl who answered to bring two cups of tea and some cakes.

"I don't quite know how I came to suspect what I came here about," she said. "But all last week, once I began to have doubts about how much money he had taken from his pay, I just couldn't get it out of my mind. I didn't even go to the Education Office as I ought to have done, until this morning. Whatever I began to think about, it all turned back to this."

"That I can well understand," he said kindly.

"When I looked at the passbook this morning I felt sure about the rest, and though it was a shock it came like a breath of fresh air. I stopped hesitating and made up my mind to act, to come here to see you. If there's anything wrong, I beg of you to tell me, so that I can feel sure of myself and know what to do. I can't bear uncertainty."

The solicitor was in a dilemma and had to think quickly. If she had found out one act of dishonesty, it wouldn't hurt her so much to learn of another. "There's sense in what you say. It would be better to let you know, though I would never have told you of my own accord."

"I believe that," she said sincerely.

"There was something wrong in his accounts," he said. "Nothing very much, but he hadn't entered three payments by an old lady . . . something just over £20."

"Are you sure of that?"

"Perfectly sure. And can I tell you something?"

She nodded, feeling in control of herself now.

"It wasn't for himself he took the money or I would have spotted it earlier. It only happened recently, and it's quite clear that he took it to go away with Mrs Amred. That's why he took your money too. You wouldn't say that it was characteristic of him?"

"No."

"I wouldn't worry too much about it. It's merely a part of something much more important. I know that his dishonesty touches you to the quick, but fundamentally he wasn't a dishonest man."

"But he acted dishonestly."

"Yes, for someone else's sake."

She made no answer to this, rose up, and then said, "Thank you very much. I'll pay back every penny of it as soon as I'm settled."

"Nothing of the kind," he said. "We get used to this kind of thing happening now and then."

"I'd prefer to pay, just for my own peace of mind."

"I won't hear of it," he insisted.

As he accompanied her through the outer office to the door, Loti Owen looked up and said, "Good afternoon."

I must write all this down if I'm to go on living. My mind is all of a turmoil. Compared with this, Iolo's running away is a mere nothing. Not a moment of peace, day or night, since going to the bank. To think that the man I trusted completely should take the money I saved so carefully by taking a lodger, doing it just for another woman, and cheating his employer as well. I could half-understand his being attracted by another woman, and I remember now his telling me during our courtship that he was always capable of doing something foolish,

52

such as giving up his job for no reason. But to steal . . . yes, that's what it is . . . is beyond my comprehension, stealing from the last person he ought to.

Here I am, in this small attic, for I couldn't think of sleeping in the room I had shared with him, and I'm glad Loti Owen's coming here compelled me to move. A fine summer night, cool in the darkness, the air perfumed from the garden, the little girl sleeping by my side. She has kicked off the bedclothes, her face all innocence. There may also be in it the possibility of something very different. She will forget her father . . . I hope so. But Rhys won't, at least he won't forget all this trouble. He follows me about everywhere like a faithful dog: he's a problem and I don't know what to do with him. I thought that when we all went to the pictures and had that special supper afterwards he was coming to himself again . . . how happy we were then compared with today!

My mind wanders here and there, always coming back to the same point, trying to find out the reason, unable to succeed because Iolo isn't here to answer for himself. If he were honest enough, he would tell me. All that talk and gossip the first few days after he had gone, everybody trying to account for it, as if that could be any kind of explanation to me who had lived with him all these years and thought she knew him. Perhaps Uncle Edward was more honest than any of us, speaking his mind and saying quite bluntly why he had never come near me after we were married. The shopkeeper and his wife were the wisest and kindest of all, talking to me and giving me a cup of coffee. And there was I, talking as much as anybody just to stifle my thoughts, which was how it had to be, for I was so unprepared for it all. What if I had suspected his friendship with Mrs Amred? But that doesn't help. Perhaps it's doubtful whether I have the capacity to suspect. But if you've given your trust once and for all, why doubt?

That raises another question, whether trusting someone means being indifferent. Maybe I thought Iolo would never be false to me simply because I had such a good opinion of myself, feeling in my heart, "He'd never do

53

that to me": I'm 38 and in my prime. When I was 21 I looked forward to reaching this age and thought that I'd like always to stay there, strong of mind and body, enough experience to tackle anything I wanted to, without making the mistakes of my youth, that life would be tranquil because I had mastered my own mind. What a hope!

But here I go, wandering off again. What if I had suspected, had noticed? Our life would not have been one of peace but of quarrelling, fault-finding, living in a turmoil, the children suffering, and in the end, the same running away. But then I'd have been prepared for it, and it's the sudden shock that's so terrible. Was there any reason for this concealment other than the nature of the man; was it really part of his make-up, this lack of frankness? A silly remark, really, as if a married man would want to parade his infidelity. Am I to blame for this habit of his of keeping things to himself, his fear of being judged? He must have known there was no justification for it. Would another woman have been kinder, more sympathetic? Was he afraid of the verdict, or was concealment the essence of his character? Here I am, asking all these questions about a man I've lived with for nearly twelve years, questions I can't answer, unable to be sure how I'd behave. We don't know ourselves, and what frightens me is that I could have lived so close to Iolo that I could read his mind, and yet he was making love to another woman. It frightens me, but it doesn't hurt me. What really hurts is that he stole my savings.

What a difference three weeks has made...A house full of different people, and yet the same number. Next week I shall be teaching again, and another woman will be cleaning the house.

VIII

"How good this tea is!" said Loti, back from the office. "I feel really happy here." She tossed her short crinkly hair away from her eyes, looking at the cakes on the table.

"Yes," said Annie. "But we mustn't expect to do so well every day now that Mrs Ffennig's out working."

"Good enough for me, anyway," said Loti over her salad. "And what I appreciate is the comfort, and her generous ways."

"I can't understand why your old landlady wouldn't think of doing more for you, looking to the future."

"What future?"

"Suppose you got married, or moved away?"

"She knew well enough that would never happen. And she's as mean as they're made."

"How do you know you won't get a better job away from here, or meet a man you really like?"

"It isn't likely . . . I haven't the wish for either."

"Don't be so silly . . . you're not thirty yet."

"Anyway, I do want to thank you for letting me join you here."

"It's Mrs Ffennig you've got to thank."

"True enough. But you've got to put up with me until bedtime, and I feel somehow that I'm a nuisance to everybody."

"That's pure nonsense," Annie said, but this was exactly what she had feared would happen when Loti came.

"You see, Annie, if only I had a family to fall back

55

upon, I could go home now and then, and it's they who would have to put up with me."

Annie felt sorry for her at the moment and said, "Treat me as your family, but don't do it too often."

"Don't you think Mrs Ffennig looks worse than she used to?"

"Yes, as if she'd had another blow, something that has shaken her to bits."

"I think she's lovelier than ever ... I always admired that light golden hair, dark blue eyes, and skin the colour of cream, but that was all until I came here. I don't know why there's this look of suffering in her eyes."

"Of course she suffers!"

"Yes, but she's rebelling against it. Can't you see her eyes flashing, as much as to say, 'Do your worst, I'm going to live on'."

"True enough. Sometimes she looks as if the sorrow of it all is too much to bear."

"I wonder if she knows about this business at the office," Loti said.

"I don't know."

"It's after that she's looked so downcast."

"I thought the day I went to Llandudno and had tea and supper with them all when I came back she'd recovered herself. I thought she'd decided that at any rate the children should be happy."

"It was a week later I saw her in our office asking to see Mr Meurig privately, looking very worried. She left with the air of a woman who'd had a severe blow."

"No-one but Mr Meurig could have told her about the theft. I never breathed a word."

"I know you didn't," said Loti. "The woman from the country doesn't know, and she hasn't lost anything by it. I thought there might be other things as well." The suggestion was typical of her.

"What a man can do once he can do again."

"Did Esta use to come here often?"

"Nearly every day."

"She never comes now, does she?"

"She was here the night before Mrs Ffennig went to your office."

"It wouldn't surprise me if Esta knew about this philandering."

"I don't think anybody did," said Annie. "I can't make out how they managed it, but of course he was often away from home."

"And Mr Meurig was generous in giving Mrs Amred days off, perhaps for his own peace at home."

They heard the bell ring, and Rhys in the hall saying, "Come in, Mr Meurig."

"Do you think something might come of this?" asked Loti.

"What do you mean?"

"If Mrs Ffennig got a divorce, they might marry."

"Nonsense, Loti!"

"Stranger things happen."

"It's not for us to decide," said Annie as she took up her book.

In the kitchen, Mr Meurig apologised for calling about a private matter: he seemed disturbed, not calm and collected as he did in the office. Lora sent the children out.

"I was thinking that you ought to get a maintenance allowance from your husband," he said.

When he said "your husband" Lora felt he was referring to a stranger, and she realised that that was how it would be, Iolo becoming more and more of a stranger. To Mr Meurig, perhaps, he was now merely someone who had done him a wrong, rather than a former employee. These thoughts flashed through her mind before he asked her, "Have you thought about it at all?"

"It never entered my mind."

"What if you had four children and couldn't earn money to keep them?"

"I'd manage somehow. But how could Iolo be found?"

"It shouldn't be difficult unless he's changed his name and got a new insurance card. He ought to contribute towards your keep, you and the children."

"Maybe, but that's no reason why I should ask for it."

"You know best," he replied, thinking her a fool.

"Reducing it all to a matter of buying and selling," she said.

"So is everything nowadays."

"If Iolo had any feeling in the matter, he'd send it without my asking," she said turning towards the fire. "But what's the use of talking? If he'd had any, he wouldn't have left me."

He admired her for not wanting revenge, and gave expression to his feeling by saying somewhat clumsily, "Yes. I suppose that's what it would amount to." He couldn't understand this lack of desire for revenge, for it played a large part in his professional life.

"It isn't quite that," she said. "Did you understand the old people who refused to go on the parish?"

He felt that this was not the way to get to know her, and when Esta came in through the back door he was glad of an excuse to go, merely saying to her, "Think it over."

Lora could have cursed the fate that brought her sister-in-law there that moment. Esta looked less sulky than the last time she came, but more nervous, afraid almost. Rarely could she behave naturally. Always acting a part before an audience, and clumsily at that. She never sat on a chair but slumped into it. Tonight she was less at ease than ever.

"You look as if you'd had a shock," she said to Lora.

"If I've had one, it wasn't now."

"I thought you looked more upset than when I last saw you," said Esta after a short silence. But for her anger at Esta's insensitivity, Lora could have laughed at so ridiculous a remark.

"Maybe," said Lora. "One thing comes on top of another. Mr Meurig just came in to suggest that Iolo ought to pay something towards our keep." She was glad to be able to be so blunt.

Esta blushed and asked if Lora knew where Iolo was.

"No I don't," said Lora. "Do you? But it wouldn't be

hard to find out, with all these cards you have to have nowadays."

"But he'll have to get a job."

"He'll do that as easily as I did. So long as I can work, I don't want anything from anybody. I'd be too ashamed to accept his charity."

"Couldn't your sister help you until you get your salary?" Esta asked, avoiding comment on the last remark.

Lora looked at her on the point of asking her if she had lost her wits, but realised that she was only talking for the sake of talking, not really knowing what to say.

"Of course she can't, with Owen so ill, and three children to bring up. I'm not worrying . . . the shops will give me credit. One of them told me so a fortnight ago."

"Good," said Esta formally.

It was in such formalities of speech that Lora saw the essential meanness of her sister-in-law. Even her "thank you" seemed to come out of the corner of her mouth, harsh and vulgar. She looked forward to telling Esta that the director of education had promised her a place in a school immediately; but that would be rubbing salt on a wound to Esta, whose ambition had always been to become a teacher. She remembered one bitch of a woman saying that when Esta got a job as secretary to a headmistress she would enjoy it because it was the next best thing to being a teacher and would give her a chance to be meddlesome.

"Would you like mother and me to take Derith off your hands for a spell? It would make things easier for you," said Esta.

"Kind of you, but I think she ought to stay with me . . . she's a bit of a bother nowadays, too young to understand what has happened, rebellious and enjoying it. She'll get more sensible, and luckily her school is next door to mine."

"When are you coming to see us?" asked Esta.

"When is your mother coming here?"

"This has taken a lot out of her, and I can't get her to move."

"I could say the same."

"She's much older than you."

"Sixty isn't old these days, and she used to go about everywhere a month ago."

"I'll tell her."

"I've got a week before school begins."

There was little more Esta could say, and she was glad to escape.

When Lora went into the parlour to clear the tea table, she found the two lodgers sitting there in silence, one reading, the other knitting. Looking for Derith to get her ready for bed, she found she wasn't with the other children, and Rhys told her that she had gone with Esta. She sent Rhys to fetch her back. She wasn't going to begin giving way.

People are getting more and more difficult to under-stand. No wonder they worship an immutable God. Until today, I'd never have thought that Miss Lloyd could have looked so sour...first time since coming here. As for the other one, I don't know. Come to think of it, Miss Lloyd didn't seem over-enthusiastic the night I suggested Miss Owen might come here, and yet they used to be great friends. It seems that the closer we get, the more we grate upon one another. And as for Esta, I couldn't make top nor tail of her, she didn't know what to do with her hands or her voice. It looks as if losing Iolo has deprived her of her background, or at least of someone she modelled herself upon. I often noticed that she was much more natural when he was about than when I was alone with her. She's as stubborn as he was, getting his own way by saying nothing, moving his chin sideways, his teeth clenched.

That stubbornness defeated me...you can't fight si-lence. She wanted to take Derith home with her tonight, but I'm not giving way to her, I don't want the child to be influenced by her. Why am I so inquisitive these days, like a ferret after a rabbit, failing to find it, but finding lots of others things! What a heap of them I'll have before

long! Will I be any the better for it, as the world is when
rid of its monsters? I've had moments of happiness when
my mind was free from doubts: that may be the only
way.

But I do get some relief by writing all this. Too many
people in the house, all on top of me, and although I'm
up in the attic, the air seems freer here. It's only here
that I can talk to myself. But I must try to sleep. How
lucky they are whose simple creed is that God is taking
care of them!

IX

Lora walked round the farm buildings at their old home
where her sister now lived. She came by the school bus
at tea time, and it was now nearly time for Owen to
come home from the quarry. In the distance she could
hear the voices of the children as they played about
the byres and the sheds: she could have sworn that
they were those of her own brothers and sisters twenty-
five years ago, the same register, the same quality. She
walked head down as if looking for something she had
lost. Not searching for part of her own childhood—
memories came flooding over her—but just testing her
memory. Here, at the head of the stone steps leading
from the yard to the byre there should be that smooth
slab. And there, the hook sticking out of the wall, and
on the gatepost, her name and Iolo's carved with a
penknife. Sure enough, there they all were; it was just
like a sum coming out right.

The standing for the rick was already there, a thick
foundation of heather. She stood on it, hearing it
crackle, inhaling the clean dry smell of it, her mind

reaching forward to winter and the pale smoke rising out of the chimney. The branches of the trees surrounding the yard loomed heavily, dark as a thunder cloud. The men had scythed the headlands ready for the cutter tomorrow, and the swathes scented the air. Between the byre and the field the little brook trickled into the bucket below, just as it did when her father and mother were alive. By the end of the week the byre would be full of hay, rustling like silk, and then silence over all. Wisps of hay moving in the wind as they trimmed the top of the stack. The grindstone was still there, so little changed because so rarely used nowadays. She came down the steps to the back of the house, bending her head instinctively as she went through the door. It might have been the very same cobweb that was there twenty-five years ago, the same bit of slate sticking out of the wall to hold a candle.

The same dust on the cow stalls, the runnels dry as always in summer. She remembered her fears when a rat scraped the wall or rustled in the hay. The greater terror when it flashed into sight and then disappeared into a hole, its tail longer than its body. And the scores of kittens born in the hay in the corner, their mother so proud of them suckling, showing her teats, and then someone cruelly putting the kittens into a bucket. The smooth noses and rough tongues of the calves, the cow's three days of longing for her calf, the calf mooing in the slaughterhouse. The hens clustered close in winter, heads in their feathers when she was sent in the dusk to shut them up. Bees in the earth wall, their monotone lasting for days after someone had broken up the nest, walls covered with heather in bloom, gorse and bilberries. She went to see if there were any berries, but found nothing but the red flowers. The children were playing in the hay, tossing the swathes as they burrowed under them. She was glad to see Rhys enjoying himself with the others, Margiad having put a horse-collar of hay round his neck.

She walked away from the house towards the mountain path to meet Owen, remembering how she used to go to meet her father when she was Derith's age so as to carry his food tin for the last hundred yards, and how she liked swinging it back and forth like the school bell. The hillside above Bryn Terfyn was always thick with feathers and dirt from hens, geese and sheep, and old tin cans that had been there for years. She remembered how she used to clear a little corner for herself in this wilderness to sit in and sew clothes for her doll.

She saw Owen approaching, tired and dragging his feet, leaning awhile on the gatepost, looking worse than when she last saw him, short of breath, perspiration running down his face.

"Not so good," was his answer to Lora's question. "I'll soon have to give up going to the quarry."

"The sooner the better. A real rest and good nourishing food will put you right."

"True, but I've got to get money for the children."

"I could help a bit—I'll soon be earning money."

"You've enough of a burden as it is, dear Lora."

His friendly look brought tears to her eyes. So frank a face, she thought, could never be other than it was when first she met him, that of a man to whom you could trust your life.

"You look a bit peaky, too," he said. "But it's a wonder you're as well as you are." This with such kindness in his voice that she unburdened herself of all her troubles regardless of how he would respond.

"My goodness, it's we who ought to help you," he said. "You've been through a lot since we last met."

"I'll be all right if my health holds ... I'll manage."

"Does anyone else know the whole story?"

"Only Mr Meurig, so far as I'm concerned. Not because he's a friend but simply because he was bound to find out some of it even if I hadn't told him the rest."

"I don't think he'd tell anyone ... he's a man of good repute in the town."

"Forgive me for pouring out all my woes like this, but I had to confide in someone. I couldn't tell Jane just now. You tell her. She'd only run him down and I couldn't bear that."

"I understand. The past means something to you."

"Yes, although I can't link it up with the future. It hurts now, and pain makes you crave for sympathy. I don't get that from Mr Meurig; he's kind enough, but to him it's all part of a solicitor's life."

"Does Esta know all this?"

"No, and she won't from me. She's of the same breed, but she's as hard as flint. Never even said she's sorry for me, and her mother has never come near me. The two of them think it's *they* who've had a blow, not me."

"Heavens above! I can't understand people."

The children ran to say food was ready. Eight of them sat at table in her mother's kitchen, just as it used to be.

Pickled herring and new potatoes, butter, bread, and oatcakes. Owen looked better after he had washed and changed his jacket, and was enjoying his food. Next to Lora sat little Now*, a comic lump of a lad, the same age as Derith, his hair sticking out like a scrubbing brush, staring at Lora until she saw him looking, then laughing and leaning his head on Margiad's arm. She was a tall gangling lass, with a wide mouth, strong white teeth, her eyes half open. They'll open some day, Lora thought, and attract some boy, with her lovely mouth and skin like cream. Her auburn hair in a tangle round her head, but the day would come when her pride would bring order into it. Guto was a shy little boy, sitting next to his mother, too shy almost to lift his head, very like Rhys to look at, fair-haired with dark blue eyes. Jane seemed happy enough in the middle of them all, very like Lora except that she was shorter and fatter.

"Now then, Now," said his father.

Now roared with laughter, and that set off all the others.

"Nothing to laugh at," said Owen.

"It's you saying the same thing twice," replied Now. They laughed away until Jane asked Lora when she

*Now is the Welsh diminutive for Owen

had last seen Uncle Edward.

"I haven't seen him since he called to ask me to housekeep for him."

"He's a strange creature," said Jane. "I called there the other day and found him in poor shape, and yet he keeps on doing the housework, living on porridge and buttermilk and suchlike. I took him some new potatoes and buttermilk, and that made him so happy. I'm sure he'd eaten it all before I got home."

"It's too late for me to go there this evening, isn't it?" said Lora.

"Better come some Saturday afternoon. He might be in bed now . . . he talks about taking his bed downstairs and letting the rest go."

"The house is too big for him. Why did he buy it?"

"It would be all right if he had a wife," said Owen.

"Don't mention women to him. He thinks they cause all the trouble in this world," said Jane.

"He likes Auntie Lora," said Now.

"How do you know?" asked his mother.

"Now runs all his errands for him," Owen explained.

"And he says it's a pity she ever married that scoundrel," said Now.

The family looked sternly at him and he began to cry.

"Look, Now," said Lora. "Never you mind. It isn't your fault he's so old-fashioned and sharp-tongued."

"He's got a moustache like a cat," said Derith. They all laughed except Now.

"Don't break your heart, Now," said Lora. "We all make mistakes. Your father and mother have made worse ones in their day." She dried his eyes with her handkerchief.

"What a lovely scent!" he said.

"Is it? Finish your herring." Her calm way with him brought him back to himself again.

"Talking of buttermilk," said Lora, "do you remember how we used to drink it at mealtimes out of the bowls with the blue and white bands round them? You never see them nowadays."

65

"There's one here somewhere," said Jane, and Now ran into the dairy and put it before Lora.

"Drink out of that," he said, and she poured the buttermilk from her glass into the bowl.

"Tastes better," said Lora.

"Can Auntie Lora take it home with her?" Now asked.

"Yes, can she?" said Guto, who hadn't said a word before.

"Of course she can."

Lora noticed that Rhys had a faraway look throughout the meal, sipping his buttermilk, looking at a spot on the cloth. She knew he didn't feel he belonged and that his laughter was all pretence. He had blushed when Now said the wrong thing, but beamed with delight when the bowl was given to his mother.

The meal ended with an old-fashioned rice pudding, more eggs than rice in it. Then Margiad came to Lora and asked if she could have some of that scent when she came to see her.

"Yes, of course. You can keep this handkerchief." Margiad tucked it into her frock.

They walked across the common, a long string of them, to wait for the bus, and when Lora entered it, leaving behind the Bryn Terfyn family, she felt cold and somehow deprived.

"I think Auntie Lora's the prettiest woman in the world," said Guto shyly as they walked home.

"So do I," said Margiad. "And she's promised me a bottle of scent."

"She's kind, too," said Now. "Uncle Edward says there's no-one like her."

As Lora and her children neared home, Derith said, "I like Now, but his hair is very ugly."

"Wasn't the food good!" said Rhys. "And I like Uncle Owen."

"It's Margiad you really like," said Derith.

"Gosh! She's got strong arms."

"Where did you hear that word?" asked Lora.

"Everybody says it," he replied.

"I saw Margiad kissing you," said Derith.

"She did it, not me. I didn't like the way she grabbed my head as if I was a horse."

"You're too touchy," said Lora. "You've got to learn to take a knock or two."

"Not from girls."

When they reached their street in the haze of a summer evening the children were still talking of their outing. Lora thought of it too, but not so vividly as to want to return. For them, it was an earnest of something that would recur again and again. For her, however, it was a treasure chest to be locked up and forgotten. All the life she had been re-living this afternoon was just like a photograph of the period: double collars, high lapels, tight trousers and short jackets. There they were, stock still, having lived, and yet not living, touching no chord within her, her own longings dying into stagnation. Some day the picture on the card would fade into dimness and she would be unable to recall them to mind.

Tonight, on the pavement, something stirred within her, something hard to define. She was all eagerness to go in, put the children to bed and sit down to write in her diary. There she would find herself, the real self of today, the only self, who had survived what she thought only happened to other people in the newspapers. Now she was going to meet her true self and confide in herself, and the vision made her hurry to overtake this new self.

She decided to go in through the back door, looked in at the kitchen as she passed the window and found it comfortless, abandoned almost, yet as if it were waiting for her. The fire was low, the cat curled up on the cushion, and on the table a tray with tea things on it. She hadn't left it there, and it gave her a moment of shock from which she soon recovered. Loti and Annie came in to explain the presence of the tray; they thought she would like a cup of tea when she came home. They also said that her mother-in-law had called when she was out. Lora frowned and said angrily, "I told Esta I was going to see my sister. Wait a minute...I'll put Derith to bed and come and join you."

Rhys took a book and went up to his bedroom, followed his mother to the attic and hung about her, and Lora knew he had read her face in the kitchen. She turned towards him quickly and said to him, "Go to your room to read and stop worrying about me. I can look after myself. We'll go and live in the country."

"Will we really?"

"Yes, some day." He went to his room whistling cheerfully.

Loti and Annie were waiting for her and had made the tea.

"My sister gave me some farm butter," Lora said. "We'll have it on these oatcakes." They talked away, the two young women determined to look after her until she went to sleep, knowing there was more trouble in store for her. Before she came, they had debated whether to tell her what her mother-in-law had said, or to leave her in ignorance.

As soon as she had seen that Lora was not there (a fact she was already aware of) she had turned on her heels scornfully and said, "Isn't she lucky to be able to gad about so soon." This was too much for Loti, who had told her that Lora had gone off with her children, and not with any other woman's husband. Annie was angry with Loti for this display of bad manners. After all, she had only been here a week or two, yet taking such a liberty. She herself could never have said it, but after all she was glad the mother-in-law had heard the plain truth. Not that it would do any good. Truth was of no concern to people like her.

Although I enjoyed the company of the two girls, I was longing to get away to bed to write this down. It's this very minute that counts, not the next one. It was when I heard that my mother-in-law had called that I should have put down what was in my mind. I couldn't say to them "that old bitch"...for that was what she was ... calling here when she knew for certain that I would be out. The true meaning of the word dawned upon me tonight when I realised her deceitfulness, for now she can say that she called and did her duty by me. How I wish I could rid myself of things without worrying about them! If I had done what Iolo did, she and her daughter might have shown more sympathy for me, but it would only be behind my back, just to show how poor a creature I was. But because their idol Iolo was at fault, their behaviour towards me must turn into some kind of jealousy. I am sure that they are furious because this act of folly was his, and not mine, and I am tempted now by this: should I keep to myself what they don't know? Hard to restrain from using a weapon that would completely floor them, but it isn't right to hold in your hand something so potent that could be used thoughtlessly. It wouldn't do anyone any good, people are only interesting when they are in control of themselves. I must keep it to myself, and that will be my burden day and night. Things keep on happening. Life used to be quiet enough. I can't say I was ever fond of Iolo's family, but I could put up with them. By now I can neither tolerate them nor quarrel with them, but I can't be mistress of my tongue for ever. I'm not enough of a psychologist to understand why my in-laws behave as they do.

I thought I'd feel better after telling Owen tonight, and for a while I did. I was so glad that he said nothing nasty about Iolo, nor did he smother me with sympathy, just listening wisely and showing that he understood. I enjoyed myself for a while, and the children behaved splendidly in spite of that awkward moment over Now's mistake. But why does my mind insist on leaping forward and imagine them turning into people like my mother-in-law? Iolo's behaviour saddens me, hers makes me furious and rouses a host of evil spirits within me. Would they have preferred a wife for him who took less trouble over his comfort? Esta dresses well because she gets a good salary, not because she has natural good taste.

Next week I start school, and it's strange how little it bothers me, this total change in my way of life. It's not that I'm thinking about: my mind hovers round one spot, like a moth about a lamp.

X

They came to the kitchen every night, for varying reasons. Annie Lloyd wearied by Loti's talking if the weather was bad and kept them indoors, Mr Meurig tired of a silent house, for he was no golfer and not given to walking and never saw the woman who worked for him once supper was over. Loti, perhaps, was the only one who did so for Lora's sake. No doubt the others persuaded themselves they were welcome there and helped Lora to forget. They did not, however, for her mind was set on one thing only in spite of the conversation, which had little more effect than a shot fired over a crowd to frighten it. Sometimes, indeed, she found herself saying one thing and thinking of something else, by now characteristic of her life. Part of it consisted of her thoughts and her diary, part of it her daily work and contacts with other people: the first dark and profound as if she lived in a cave, the other light and shallow. In the latter she was restless, moving here and there like a bird on the wing, solitary. Occasionally there was a change when she met Owen and shared her confidences with him, but that rarely happened, and it carried her no further forward, just going round and round on the same ground, finding nothing new. Although she dreaded discovering another instance of Iolo's dishonesty nothing came to light, and by now she thought Mr Meurig was right in saying that he stole merely to carry on with Mrs Amred.

When she discussed the matter with Owen he listened patiently, but it dawned upon her that he was getting tired of her persistence, and that she was forgetting that illness brought him troubles of his own. As for Mr Meurig, she never spoke to him about it again: it was only by accident, in a moment of stress, that the matter of the bank passbook came to his knowledge, and as she did not know him well, to talk about it would not comfort her. But if he were really a friend...

Bordering on this aspect of her life there was another, in the relationship between her and Esta and her mother-in-law. Although they did not know as much as she did, Iolo's disappearance grieved them both, but it was something they could not share; it brought a gap between them that must either widen or close, probably the latter. She felt that any discussion could only take place across the image of Iolo standing between them.

It was on one of these nights, the rain pouring down, that Esta came in. The four of them were playing cards because conversation proved impossible. Lora hated cards, and indeed every other game since she grew up: she couldn't understand how anyone could get any pleasure from using his skill to beat another, and it was out of courtesy that she played tonight; it took all her strength of mind to do so.

They were laughing over a story Mr Meurig told them about an old man from up country who came to him one day to make his will, and instead of naming those who were to inherit, he insisted on giving the names of those who would not. "So-and-so nothing, so-and-so, nothing." It was worthwhile paying for the privilege of telling the rogues how near they came to inheriting. And that was how Esta found them when she came in by the back door. Lora offered to let her take her place at cards, but she refused, nor would she take a cup of tea... she said she couldn't stay. Lora wondered why she came, took her to the door and asked if there was anything she wanted. No, she had just called, that's all. "You've got company, I see," she said, and went out without a smile and without wishing the others goodnight.

"Isn't she a sour-face?" asked Mr Meurig. "Is she like that in school?"

"Not when Miss Immanuel is about."

"I don't know how Mrs Ffennig puts up with her."

"That's just about what she does," said Loti.

"I'm afraid I've upset your sister-in-law," he said to Lora when she came in.

"Oh no . . . it wasn't you . . . she's been like that for some time," said Lora, exchanging a glance of understanding with him.

They dispersed, Loti and Annie to their own room, leaving the two others in the kitchen, the sound of laughter having given way to silence, a lack of desire for speech. Lora bit her lip, wondering whether he could succeed in breaking through this wall of self-defence she had built round herself.

"Do you mean that your sister-in-law is always like this when she comes here?" he asked.

"She's changed totally since Iolo went off."

"You were very friendly before that, weren't you? Going about together . . ."

"Yes, but . . ."

"It's presumptuous of me to ask questions."

"Not at all. It's just that I can't explain properly. As Iolo's sister I was naturally glad to see her here and to go away with her and so on. But I couldn't say I regarded her as a real friend."

"Could you confide in her?"

"About Iolo and myself and family matters, yes. But I don't think I could bare myself to her, even then. I could never discuss religion, or my feelings about people I love."

"Have you no-one you could talk about things like that with? Pardon me for behaving like a solicitor!"

"Don't apologise. It does me good to talk like this. I've got into a groove of living and thinking, and I'd

72

better try to forget my troubles and think of something else. I can't forget them entirely, of course, but talking to a friend may help."

"True, and a friend could change the aspect of things and help you to look differently on your troubles."

"It doesn't seem likely now. I do have a friend, but she's in London and we only meet once a year. You can't deal with something like this in a letter."

"No, the words seem to change and grow cold."

"You can't even write it down to begin with. Don't forget, I didn't live here until we got married, and the only person I knew was my sister-in-law."

"So of course you became friends."

"Yes, friends of a kind."

"It's a pity in a way that she came between you and some other woman you could have made a friend of. I'm sure she was glad enough to go about with so attractive a woman." If Lora had not been so angry after seeing Esta off, she would have felt she was blushing.

"I don't think you can make many friends after marriage," she said. "You've got your husband, and you tell him everything. There's no room for anyone else, especially if you've got children."

He thought that Iolo had found plenty of room for other affairs, but all he said was, "Everybody doesn't think that, but obviously your family completely filled your life."

"I took no pleasure in anything else, and had no money to travel."

He found something rather naïve in this remark, but he didn't know that it was exactly this that gave her husband such a hold over her, for he took little interest in the house, garden, children, or in trying to improve his position. Meurig could not take his eyes off the silken waves of hair that covered her head, the profile he had seen when she had drawn the curtains between her and the world on the night her husband left.

"Have you ever thought of going somewhere else to live?" he asked.

"No, I haven't. I couldn't easily go now I've got a job here. And of course Iolo may come back."

And that was the last thing he expected her to say.

* * *

When they got to the parlour Loti said, "Did you ever see such manners?"

"What ... that Esta?"

"Yes."

"I never saw the like. I'm afraid there's a lot of gossip in school. She and that Miss Davies who lodges across the road are at it whenever they get a chance."

"I wouldn't be surprised if she keeps watch on who comes here, or on Mr Meurig. There was a time when she was after him, coming to the office, changing her will a score of times just as an excuse for coming."

"I wouldn't be a bit surprised," said Annie. "But I hope Mrs Ffennig doesn't think I've been gossiping."

"She wouldn't think anything of the kind. Between you and me, I think she's very innocent in some ways ... one of the 'think no evil' type. She isn't suspicious enough. If she'd suspected her husband a bit more she wouldn't be in this mess now."

"But Loti, if she'd begun to suspect, it would have been a cat and dog life."

"That might have helped her to bear all this ... at the very least she'd have been prepared for it."

"But what about the children?"

"So would they. Bad for them at the time, of course. I think Rhys has had a terrible shock, and he's fretting. Have you noticed how he clings to her?"

"Yes, I have."

"How he went off to bed last night when we went in the kitchen, looking as if he was afraid we were going to take her away from him?"

"I didn't see that."

"What a strange world this is, Annie! Two months ago you were here, quiet and contented, and I was with Mrs Jones, quiet and unhappy. And now we two are

74

happy together, with a drama being played all round us."

"I don't like my part in it."

"What part's that?"

"The character under suspicion."

"If you don't get suspected of anything worse than tale-telling to Esta, you deserve a bang on the head for worrying."

"Have you noticed how she always walks looking down at her feet?" Annie asked.

"Yes and they're not worth looking at, but it saves her from looking people in the face."

Annie laughed at this.

"What are you laughing at?"

"How well it describes her. And her brother too."

"No, I don't agree there. I've been watching him in the office. He was well thought of because he could keep his mouth shut, but he wasn't like that really. Though talkative people are often mis-judged, for that matter."

"They're not always straight. But what were you going to say about Iolo?"

"He was supposed to be a good worker, but I noticed some time ago he was only giving the impression. His books aren't well kept, you know. There's another thing too. He spoke as if he was well read, but he wasn't really. Just making a show of what he saw in the news-paper headlines."

"And Esta repeating the same performance among intelligent people."

"Where was that?"

"In that English society devoted to the arts."

"Mr Meurig is a likeable man, isn't he?" said Annie, changing the subject.

"An excellent employer, but I wouldn't like him for a husband."

"He's not likely to ask you."

"That's not the point. I was trying to say that an excellent man isn't always likeable."

"What's wrong with him?"

"I can't really say, but I feel no nearer to him now than I did five years ago."

"Distant?"

"Yes."

"But there was something likeable about the way he told that story tonight."

"Yes, the first time I saw him so relaxed."

They heard Mrs Ffennig on her way to bed, and stopped talking.

Seeing the light under Rhys's door, Lora went in and found him lying on his back, his hands behind his head, staring at the ceiling.

"Why are you still awake?" she asked.

"It's too hot. What were you laughing at?"

"Mr Meurig was telling us a funny story about an old man."

The boy's face gave nothing away. Although he took after his mother in looks, at this moment he was like his father in one of his shut-in moods.

"What did Mr Meurig want?"

"He just came for a chat, and then Miss Lloyd and Miss Owen came to the kitchen and we had a game of cards."

"Who won?"

"Nobody . . . we didn't finish it. Aunt Esta came in."

"What did she want?"

"I've no idea. She went away quickly. Just paying a call. I think she was shocked at finding so many of us here."

"She was just snooping."

"Maybe."

"Tell me, Mam, do you like Mr Meurig?"

"I don't know. He's very kind, but I've never thought about whether or not I like him. Why do you ask?"

"The boys in school are teasing me and saying I'll have another father."

"And you've been worrying about that, haven't you? I told you to take no notice if children tease you."

"I'm not really worrying. It's just that I thought if you liked him, I'd like him too."

"Don't be silly. Your father is your father, and my husband, and I couldn't take another man for my husband. Your father isn't dead, remember, and he may come back some day."

"I don't want him to come back."

"You mustn't talk like that." He began to cry, and she comforted him.

She felt sorry for the boy: he had just won a scholarship to the grammar school and no-one had taken any notice of it. If it hadn't been for these troubles they'd have celebrated it somehow or other.

"Listen Rhys," she said brightly. "Tell me what bothers you most."

"I'm afraid you're worrying."

"Of course I am. It would be strange if I didn't."

"But you didn't suffer like this when grandad and grandma died."

"That was different. I had your father then."

"You've got mè now."

"Yes, I have, but you're not old enough to understand everything."

"When will I be?"

"I don't know. By then you'll have forgotten about him and you'll be thinking of someone else."

"Who?"

"Some girl," she said, laughing.

"I won't. Girls are no good."

"Your mother was a girl once."

"I like you better as you are."

"I won't always be like this."

"Don't say that!"

"It's true. Anyway, we all want this trouble over, don't we?"

"Yes, of course."

"Well, I'll have changed, you'll be grown up, a young man, and nothing will be the same as it was."

"Pity about that."

"Maybe, but it's got to come. You wouldn't like not to grow up and always be a little boy, people staring at you, would you?"

"No, I wouldn't."

"That's that then, so what about a cup of tea in bed?"

He brightened. "Yes if you'll have one with me."

Lora went down and brought up a tray with bread and butter.

"This is the best treat we've ever had, isn't it? I'll sleep after this," said Rhys.

"And promise not to worry?"

"I'll do my best."

"Would you like to leave here and go somewhere else?"

"Where to?"

"Somewhere in the country ... we could go to Uncle Edward's, there's plenty of room there."

He thought a bit and then said, "I'd have to go to school by bus."

"That's nothing," she said, and at that moment Derith's face came round the door.

"Here comes the spoil-sport," he said.

"Fair play," said his mother. "No-one bothers about her from one week to another."

"I want to join this tea party by night," she said.

"You can have some milk," said Lora, and went down to the kitchen for it. When she returned, Derith was sitting on Rhys's bed eating his bread and butter. There they sat, the three of them in silence, and Lora felt that in spite of all the suffering it was in their company she was happiest. Elsewhere, she had no sense of contact. Her mind was too unsettled for her to sit down and write after going up to her room, so she put Derith to bed and sat by her side. "That was a nice tea party," the child said as she fell asleep.

Lora thought over the events of the evening. Obviously, people were talking because Mr Meurig was visiting her. She must be careful, for she lived in Wales, and she mustn't forget that her husband was still alive. But whatever she did, people would talk. Rhys was more of a problem ... she could deal with Mr Meurig, but how to get a boy of ten to erase from memory all that had happened was beyond her. If going to live in the country would help, go they must. The best way of helping Rhys was for her not to worry herself. She could manage that more easily if Iolo had done no more than go away, but there were other matters the boy knew nothing about.

Then there was Esta ... she was beyond understanding. Her behaviour tonight, in front of the others, had been disgraceful. Luckily she had managed to keep her temper and not let Esta see how angry she was. She wondered where she'd been living all this time, how an outsider like Mr Meurig could see that her sister-in-law had stood between her and other people. She'd been living in a fool's paradise for years, just because she thought that marriage was the be-all and end-all. It was the children who were important, and she must go out with them more often, instead of spending the evenings indoors talking.

*   *   *

Aleth Meurig sat in his parlour thinking. The room was clean and lifeless, not even a clock ticking. Something more than furniture was needed here, he thought. The light tread of a woman on the carpet, rustle of silk as she moved about giving tea or coffee to her friends, light falling on a white neck. Life did not end at forty, and his practice was so profitable that he could afford to entertain and bring some life into the house. When he left for the office of a morning, nothing but silence, pure silence. Saturday and Sunday were unbearable. Across the road, a house too full of people and children, a woman worrying about a worthless man and working hard. It was easy to see tonight that her mind was far away, thinking of one thing and saying something else, playing cards badly, innocent to the point of folly. Why had the Almighty given her such beauty, wasted in a hole of a place like this? And that last remark of hers! She would probably take back her husband when he was tired of the flibbertigibbet he had run away with, just to be respectable again, or more likely because she

79

could forgive him and forget what he had done. Keeping up some kind of life with him, going to chapel and to Sunday school with the children, living a "good life". What fools they were, the so-called "good".

There was at least this to be said for Iolo, he had broken the monotony of his life and had some kind of an affair. We are still countryfolk, he thought, and Welsh at that: the Welsh failed to enjoy their pleasures because of their religion and failed to enjoy their religion because they wanted to follow their lusts. How innocent Iolo's wife was, blindly so, admitting that she had always stayed at home, failing to see that it gave him his chance to escape. She did say that she had no money for travelling. Iolo had only imitated the wealthy, with someone else's money. Poor men can't afford to run away with other men's wives. No need for Iolo to remain poor, if only he were ambitious enough to study for his exams instead of remaining a solicitor's clerk, no need for his wife to take in lodgers ... she would be able to travel, and other people than her neighbours could admire her beauty. She might still have a chance ... old Edward Thomas had remembered her in his will, and tonight he had nearly revealed this to her. However, the old sometimes outlive the young.

He asked himself whether, deep down, what he really wanted was to have her beauty adorning his house, even though she had said that her husband might come back. Another thought struck him, that she seemed able to surround herself with a protective wall, as she did when her sister-in-law called. Perhaps she was not so innocent, perhaps she saw through them all, her husband included. All her defences were down the day she called at his office after finding that Iolo had stolen her money. That day she was a woman disappointed, thoroughly sincere. He got up and went to bed. Time would show whether she was capable of loving another man.

XI

A fine Saturday morning at the end of July, Miss Lloyd
having gone away on holiday the day before, and Miss
Owen not wanting a meal because she too was leaving
straight from the office that afternoon. Lora and the
children were looking forward to their own holidays in
a fortnight, and she decided to cut down her work and
take the children out. Luckily, the woman who came
in for a couple of hours a day when Lora was at school
was a good worker. Lora had been up at six to make
cakes and a pudding before it got too hot, and she had
made the beds and was ready to start preparing a simple meal when the door bell rang. Someone coming to
spoil our outing, she thought, but she found Margiad,
Guto and little Now standing there shyly.

"Mother asked me to give you this letter," said Margiad.

It gave her a shock, thinking surely it must be to
say that Owen was worse. However, it ran, "Dear Lora,
I hope this crowd of children doesn't disturb you, but
I had to send Margiad to the chemist's to get some
medicine the doctor had ordered for Owen. He's no
worse, I'm glad to say. Nothing would do but that Margiad must call for some bottle of scent you'd promised
her. She was too shy to ask herself, so here I am writing
this letter. And as you well understand, the others had
to come with her to your house. I wonder whether you'd
all like to come here for a week in August? Owen is
going to take an extra week off from the quarry to do
some odd jobs about the place before winter, and it will
do him good. How nice it would be if it was the week

Miss Owen goes away and then you'd feel free. Yours, Jane."

The three children stood in the hall, as shy as if it were Buckingham Palace. Someone had plastered Now's hair with oil. Margiad had tied her hair neatly at the back, and Guto looked spick and span.

"Have you done your errand, Margiad?" Lora asked.

"Done it before coming here so that we can go straight to the bus," she replied. Rhys and Derith rushed in and made a great fuss.

"We'd thought of going across the river after dinner and taking our tea with us. Let's all go! Better than going to the pictures." They all agreed.

"Margiad and Rhys, come and help me get the meal ready, and Derith and Now go and play in the garden. I wonder what Guto could do?"

"I could carry the bread and butter to the table."

"Splendid! Rhys and Margiad can wash the lettuce while I cut bread and butter."

At the table, all was silence.

"Are you like this in school?" Lora asked.

"No!" they cried.

But even that couldn't get them talking until Now, obviously feeling that children and silence didn't go together, burst out with, "Mother told us at the peril of our lives not to talk about Uncle Iolo."

They all laughed except Rhys, Lora more than anyone.

"Was that why you were so quiet, Now?" she asked.

"Yes, I was afraid of opening my mouth in case I said it."

"You're a strange boy, Now. You'll go through life putting your foot in it, but never mind." He couldn't see it, but it set them all talking.

When they were finishing their meal Esta came in through the back door, so surprised at seeing all the children that she said nothing at first. Then, in her clumsy way, she said she'd come to ask if Derith could go with her to Bangor that afternoon.

"Can I go?" the child asked.

"No," said Lora, explaining that they had all arranged to go out and take their tea with them.

"Oh well," said Esta. "You know best."

"It wouldn't be right to leave Derith out."

Derith began to cry, and Rhys looked as if he could hit her.

"That will do, Rhys. Leave her alone. She'll get over it. She can't always have her own way."

Esta hesitated as if she thought Lora might change her mind, but she didn't, and silence filled the kitchen, the Bryn Terfyn children looking as if they wanted to hide away somewhere.

"I'm trying to keep the family together, what's left of it," Lora said. "And Derith must learn she's not going to be spoilt."

"Very well then," said Esta. "I'm going."

"Would you like to join us, Esta?"

Rhys's face fell.

"No thanks," she muttered.

After she had gone they all felt embarrassed, as if they knew there was something wrong but didn't know what. Lora tried to restore the situation and to look happy. She went to wash the dishes and get tea ready. She knew Margiad was longing to go upstairs, and they went together to the attic.

"Is this where you sleep?" she asked.

"Yes, it's fine up here."

"Just like our place at home, isn't it?"

"Yes, it is." She looked for the scent bottle. "Here you are."

"Oh, isn't it lovely! What is it?" Margiad asked.

"Jasmine ... spell it out in English."

"Is this the one you like best?"

"Yes, it's the one Iolo always gave me. He gave me this last Christmas."

"Oh, but you shouldn't give me this! Haven't you got another?"

"No, I'd rather you took it. Really."

"I'll remember what scent you like best and send you a bottle as soon as I earn some money."

"Bless you!" said Lora, kissing the child, but thinking that she would have to be blunt with Esta, no matter what company was present.

"Do you long for Uncle Iolo?"

"Not so much as I would if he were dead, but it hurts more."

Margiad, not much impressed, began looking at the oddments on the dressing table while Lora changed her frock.

"Would you like to go to the bathroom?" Lora asked. "There's a clean towel on the side of the bath." This was what Margiad, a country girl, was hoping for, the joy of washing in a town house.

Derith came in looking very sad and her mother, feeling sorry for her as she always did for the defeated, told her to go to the bathroom with Margiad, who would wash her face for her. "I'll put some scent on your face," she added.

"Look, Derith," said Margiad as she dried her face. "We'll have much more fun on the beach. Ten minutes of Bangor and you'll have pains in your legs, a headache, blisters on your feet, a pain in your belly and you'd have to be carried home on a stretcher. But you can walk barefoot on the shore, paddle until your feet are smooth as velvet, lie on your face in the sun, and have a much better tea than you'd get in Bangor. On nice clean sand instead of somewhere dirty, everybody too busy to bring you a teaspoon, stewed tea, nowhere comfortable to sit, everybody bumping against you as they pass until your hat's all out of shape, flat like a soldier's cap, and you none the better for it all. Even the smell of the cakes in that basket is enough to get a sick man out of bed. And don't forget, you've got a very good mother. What would you do if she died?"

"Go to Aunt Esta."

"Don't you believe it, she wouldn't want you then."

Lora overheard this conversation as she stood in the landing and could imagine Margiad mouthing all this rigmarole. Derith came out all smiles.

"Look out!" cried Lora as she sprayed them with eau

de cologne until they screamed with delight.

The shore was not the ideal place for children, too many rocks, too little sand, but they could paddle even if they couldn't run about much. Lora spread her coat on the rocks and sat there, her legs and feet on the sand, enjoying the sun and the breeze. Out of the corner of her eye she could see the children paddling, the colour of their clothes criss-crossing in a pattern, the waves breaking quietly, the silence as they receded, voices sounding far away although they were close at hand. She banished all thought from her mind, all feeling but that of bodily existence, resting peacefully there, lulled by the sound of the sea.

Only once before had she felt like this, a spring afternoon during the war when she was tired out by anxiety about how to get food for the lodger and evacuees. She had gone upstairs to wash after dinner before going out again to search in the shops. Looking in the mirror, she found she looked like a corpse. She decided not to go out, but to make do with what was in the house. She went downstairs, made herself a drink of hot lemon, took two aspirins and put a hot water bottle in her bed. She slept like a log, and that was how the children found her when they came back from school. What was important was not to care.

It was the whispering that woke her, Margiad saying quietly, "Pity to wake her up, poor soul."

"Did you sleep?" Rhys asked.

In the house all was quiet again, her sister's children gone, Derith in bed, and Rhys on his way there. Lora was beginning to prepare Miss Owen's supper when Mr Jones, the minister called. She thought it strange that he should come on a Saturday night, but perhaps he had some important news ... about Iolo, it immediately came to her mind. But he talked about this and that without revealing the purpose of his visit, which was obviously not to enquire about her health. He kept staring at a spot on the table instead of meeting her eyes, keeping his finger on it, showing that he was reluctant to come to the point.

85

"Mrs Ffennig," he said, still dithering, then turning his eyes to a spot on the arm of his chair, "I don't like saying what I have to tell you." Something about Iolo, she thought. "But I feel it my duty to let you know that people are talking about Mr Meurig coming here so often."

"So often?"

"That's what they say . . . perhaps you didn't know."

"He has every right to come here, hasn't he?"

"Of course, but you know as well as I do that once people start talking, all kinds of lies will spread."

"I never thought of that."

"A pity, for a woman like you."

"What does it matter? Truth is truth."

"In one sense it doesn't matter, but as you know, even when a lie is proved to be a lie, some slur remains, just enough to conceal the truth, and that will be people's attitude towards you."

"I suppose that's the kind of world we live in, unfortunately."

"In a different situation it wouldn't matter, but let me explain. I don't know what your plans are, nor Iolo's."

"It's nothing to do with Iolo."

"Oh yes it has. Suppose you wanted a divorce because of his deserting you, your case would be weakened if the other side raised such points against you, however untrue they were."

"But it's Iolo who left me . . . no-one can say I run after men."

"No, but you know what lawyers are. Forgive me if I've hurt you."

"You haven't."

"I mean the lawyers on the other side, glad of a chance to use such stories."

"But truth will prevail."

"Not always, even in a court of justice. Does Miss Ffennig come here often?"

"Yes, but not as often as she used to."

"Has she ever found Mr Meurig here?"

86

"Yes, once."

"Take a hint kindly, Mrs Ffennig, and forgive me for interfering, but outsiders sometimes see more than those on the inside."

"Yes," she said sadly. "But may I tell you what one who *is* on the inside feels?"

"Please be frank," he said expansively. "What else is a minister for?"

"You may not like hearing the truth."

"Better out with it."

"It's three months since Iolo went, and no-one's cared *what* happened to the children and me except Mr Meurig and the two young women who lodge here."

"Well, I agree it was natural enough for Mr Meurig to come here at first, seeing that your husband was his clerk, and a good one by all accounts."

"He's been more than a good employer. And other people might have shown their sympathy with me too and called here to see how I was. Plenty came the first week, but that was only out of curiosity."

"But it wasn't as if Mr Ffennig had died suddenly."

"It would have been just the same if he had. They all forget. Mr Meurig and the two young women come to the kitchen now and then for a game of cards, that's all. If it makes any difference, he never stays with me alone."

"The mere fact that someone has seen him come in is enough, I suppose."

"Maybe. My sister-in-law came in one evening when we were all laughing at a funny story Mr Meurig told us, and I expect she thought I was thoroughly enjoying myself."

"Doesn't one of the teachers at the school she's in live across the road?"

"So it seems. But I didn't know until yesterday."

There was an embarrassed silence.

"Forgive me if I've hurt you, Mrs Ffennig," said the minister quietly. He was on the point of going when she said, "Thank you, Mr Jones, for trying to help me. It really does help to know these things. I don't know whether you've found that people are generally one step ahead of you in your own affairs. Here I am, in all this trouble, and I'm sure other people think I've already forgotten everything. If I forget at all, it will be a long time ahead."

There was such a world of sadness in her voice that he could not tell her his message, which was that next Tuesday night, Iolo would be dismissed from membership of the chapel. After hearing her story, he decided to try to persuade the chapel elders to cancel their decision.

Loti Owen came in before he left, her supper unprepared, but she only wanted a cup of tea and a piece of bread and butter. She had it in the kitchen with Lora, and they had a long talk together.

As to my feelings, I just can't describe them, but I know it's good for me to empty my mind on paper: I can't do it on other people. The pain gets worse, not better. What is clear is that there are forces at work that I'm not conscious of. From one point of view, Mr Jones the minister was only interfering in my affairs, and if I had felt this, I'd have lost my temper and told him to mind his own business. But there was something in his tone of voice that distinguished him from the usual busy-bodies who come to you with fair words to assure you that they are only thinking of your own good when you know they've come to accuse you. He knows the truth now, whatever use he makes of it, but this kind of knowledge does harm in other ways. He suggested things that had never crossed my mind. Does Mr Meurig come here only out of sympathy? Or has he something else in mind? If he has it wouldn't draw me away from him ... it's a thrill for any woman to think a man admires her. It might stay in my mind, and goodness knows what that might lead to. A good thing Loti Owen came in when she did. What Mr Jones said was no news to her ... she seemed to have something on her mind she didn't wish to say, but she agreed that his intentions were good and that it was better for me to know. I like her when we are alone together. But the question still remains, is it best for me to know or not?

Would it have been better for me to know that Iolo was making love to Mrs Amred? The fact that I know now and didn't know then is merely due to the passage of time, and ignorance then and knowledge now are united to frighten me, knowledge and pain both increasing. How pleasant those few hours at the seaside with the children were, that bodily feeling of relaxation, emptying the mind, falling asleep, forgetting the children, much as I like them. They know little but their day-to-day delights, quick to forget their disappointments. It was only out of pure ignorance that they put their foot in it, due to their inexperience. Rhys and Margiad half-realise that I suffer, and it was only out of kindness that she put her foot in it in the bedroom, but then things happen like that. That bottle of scent meant such a lot to her: to me, when Iolo gave it to me at Christmas, very little. Today, giving it to Margiad meant nothing to me, and I gave it as casually as I am sure Iolo bought it ... I'm sure he gave Mrs Amred something more expensive. There I go, showing my jealousy. If Iolo had died, I'd have given it with all the emotion one experiences when giving to the living the possessions of someone who had died. To Margiad, it was treasure, and how she enjoyed going through my trinkets and going to a bathroom, something new to her.

While I was washing up I tried to think whether Iolo had ever given me anything of value, but I couldn't remember any. Can it be that the mere act of giving something has convinced me that we did give to one another? Heavens above! Why do I say such things even in this diary? Iolo got his own way by being silent when we disagreed about things. I can see the past more clearly now, why we seemed to be happy. One famous novelist says that love must be all on one side for a happy marriage. He must have been a cynic, and their eyes are covered with a film, like a blind man's. People who keep on giving without receiving are probably fools, and fools never learn from one another. I wonder which of them will prove the fool in this matter of Mrs Amred. Will it be her, suspecting, probing more and more? It struck me that I ought to change the locks on the doors . . . what if Iolo returned when I am away?

XII

Lora was busy tidying up the house and getting the children's clothes ready for their holiday at Bryn Terfyn. Loti had already gone and the house seemed emptier than it had been since the spring. At times like this the house seemed to develop its own personality, as unhappy as a dog whose master is leaving, the furniture so prominent, stiff as corpses under the dust sheets.

This time last year, she thought, just the same feeling of emptiness, of difference. Iolo wanted to go to Llandudno: she did not and would have preferred Bryn Terfyn, so the holiday wasn't worth what it cost. The food was poor and scarce, the service slow, nothing to do but potter about and play with the children on the beach. As she moved about the house she remembered suddenly Mrs Amred came to Llandudno to see them, and how willingly Iolo had paid for her meal. She didn't pursue the thought except to wonder how blind she had been. However, there was nothing to gain by dwelling on her obtuseness at the time. Mrs Amred didn't come into her world of suffering, it was the theft of money that hurt her, and that she could talk about in Bryn Terfyn. Owen would understand, and even if her sister said nothing about it, it was better than having Esta coming in with that air of accusation.

Everything was ready by four o'clock, and she made the tea. She felt she could put all unpleasantness behind her, like shutting the door on an empty room so as to be able to forget it and look forward to what was coming. She knew that in Bryn Terfyn she would be in another world, wearing what clothes she liked, enjoying the fresh air on the common, and best of all, no neighbours, no-one to bother about who came into the house.

A week of this would be like coming out of prison, and she hoped to be able to forget the events of the past three months. She put her diary in her bag, but did not think she would need it. Then, in the silence, the door bell rang, and she knew she looked annoyed when she opened it to Mr Meurig.

"I called to ask whether I could take you in the car to your sister's," he said.

"I'd rather not, thanks," she replied quickly.

"Why not?"

"It would only make people talk."

"It would only take fifteen minutes and save you trouble with your luggage and children on the bus. Are you going to let what people think deprive you of that comfort?"

"Please, please, give me that much peace of mind by not coming! I do thank you for offering though."

"Do you suffer all that much because of what people say?"

"I do at present."

"When is it going to stop?"

"When I care nothing about anybody."

"So you do care about some?"

"Not really, but why give them something to talk about needlessly? I'd love to if there were any grounds for it, mind."

"What are you trying to tell me?"

She shrugged. "Only that I'd be making them think something that wasn't true."

"I see," he said slowly, but thought they might not be far wrong at that.

The children came in.

"Stay and have tea with us, Mr Meurig," she said. "There's not much left, mind. I've been clearing out the pantry."

"Do you really want me to stay?" he said playfully. "What will people say?"

"Well, as you're in here now you might as well stay. This short spell won't matter."

"Thanks. It's an unexpected pleasure."

She liked him that moment because he hadn't taken offence, and for a certain boyishness about him. He was much more lonely than she was, more helpless at home, and he was so plain and straightforward in speech.

"I don't know how you can make such good food at a difficult time like this. Your children are lucky," he said.

"We won't get food like this next week," said Rhys.

"You'll get better food, my boy, plenty of farm butter and eggs and buttermilk." Rhys pulled a face.

"I'd rather go to Llandudno than to the country," said Derith.

"This time your mother is going where *she* wants to," said Lora.

"Is that so?" said Meurig.

"I'm sick of being in this huddle of houses."

"And of those who live in them?"

"Some of them. There'll be nobody watching me there."

"I hope you're right."

"What do you mean?"

"Only that this world is full of evil-minded folk."

"Lots of them will be away on holiday."

"You know the devil isn't short of apprentices."

"Solicitors ought to know," she said, and he laughed, glad to see her cheerful. As he was going out he said, as if the thought had just struck him, "Don't you think, Mrs Ffennig, that you ought to have a new lock on your front door, as you are going away?"

"I've already put one there, and on the back."

On the way home he wondered what had come over her. Was she as naïve as he thought . . . she who seemed to trust everybody, taking these precautions against her husband's return during her absence? Was it out of fear, or a desire to banish him from her world? Fear of what? Was she afraid he'd remove some of her mother's things? It wouldn't surprise him if Iolo's mother and sister knew where he was. His profession had made him familiar with the way people went about achieving their aims. It might not be a mere puritanical streak in her that made her object to a visit from him: she might be clever enough to know that such visits might be cited against her some day. As time went by, it was obvious that this affair of his housekeeper and his clerk was no mere weekend jaunt. The street would be emptier than ever this coming week.

As she ate her supper in Bryn Terfyn, Lora felt a thousand years away from that tea time in her own house, although the vision of it kept floating through her mind. Supper in this kitchen was like eating out of doors, the mountain air coming through the open doors, and although there were eight of them, and plenty of noise, she felt less confined. A vision of her mother in the corner by the fire, and she knew exactly how she'd behave if Lora had come home in the middle of all this trouble. She'd be watching her all the time, looking her in the eye to see if she was suffering. To her mother, a child's suffering was her very own, physically almost. There would be none of this in Bryn Terfyn now. Owen would sympathise with her, as would others, up to a certain point where the boundary lies between people. As for Jane, her attitude would be that the sufferer was at fault. She had no use for people like Iolo, and if he brought trouble upon her, it was her fault for marrying him. "You asked for it" was her response, and to her intuitive mind cause and effect were as yesterday and today. Iolo was like that when he married, and it was her sister's fault that she hadn't

94

discovered it. Apart from Rhys and Margiad, the children felt nothing, except that something had happened. Margiad had imagination enough to understand, up to a point. Rhys understood because his relations with his mother were so close as to make any suffering of hers his own suffering.

Once again I've reached the limit of the bearable. When I came here I did not think I'd need this diary but would forget everything and enjoy the fields, the common, the food, the wind and the smells and the views. Above all, the feeling of having come back to my family. But there's no sense of belonging . . . I've cut adrift from my own past. My sister lives in my old home. I knew they'd be kind to me in every way except the one I crave, and that is to be understood. This is all I ask, and it is impossible to get. My own fault, I know; stupid of me to expect anyone to understand, any more than I could myself understand someone else's feelings. I can see nothing ahead of me except having to lead a double life, pretending to others that I can manage, and being honest with myself only on paper. I sometimes ask myself what am I really worried about. Because Iolo loves another woman? I don't think so. I'm sure he'll soon get tired of her . . . she's an insensitive creature, and there's a touch of the poetic in Iolo. Never have I known her reveal any kind of emotion: she talks about the dead as she would about the weather, and of the weather in terms of the mortality of man.

I saw nothing in her but a pretty face, always alert. No need for me to be envious. But the ever recurring pain lies in this, that Iolo was unworthy of trust in the ordinary things of life. Easy enough to lose your head, fall in love, and later come to your senses. But trust isn't something to throw away like this. People often say "he's deceived her" when a man deserts a girl he's been courting. But when coolness comes, that isn't deceit. Deceit is what Iolo did to me, taking my money . . . not because money is important in itself, but because it represented our trust in each other. People can't see that. It shows

*that I didn't matter, and isn't that the very worst kind
of hurt, that now you're of no importance to someone
you once were? Or is it, I ask myself, because in my
inmost being I still love Iolo? We reduce everything to
what concerns us personally.*

*And what about Mr Meurig? I'm beginning to be fond
of him: he was so likeable this afternoon. Am I to keep
him away because of what people might say, although
I enjoy his company? That's the worst of living in so
narrow-minded a community. But why worry tonight,
with the sweet scent of hay from the yard, a bird singing
somewhere? Long ago I could have told you what bird
it was, but I don't know now, though it may come back
to me as a poem does. Derith's fast asleep, arms stretched
out, without a care in the world, as I was once when I
was too young to look back. Death is one of many things
I look back at today, without alarm. I wonder whether
Iolo's dishonesty will one day die away in memory. If
it does, he will no longer haunt me and I shall be free
of him. I can't imagine that such a day will ever come,
and I must persevere through all the trials and evasions
of today.*

XIII

Lora wanted to go alone to see Uncle Edward in Ty
Corniog, though she did not know why. The last time
the two of them had been alone together things had
not gone well, in fact, they had quarrelled, but since
then, she had often thought about what he had said
and about him. There was something spare and clean
about him, from his clothes to his words: the clothes

of a neat little miser, the words of an honest pagan cutting clean through the matter at issue, without frills. She would like to know him better: not easy, because like all of his kind, his miserliness drew him apart. Meeting people meant giving, and receiving. He could do without the receiving if he did not have to give. It was only from his sister, her own mother, that he was content to receive, because she was one who gave as readily to a miser as to a spendthrift. Her last encounter with him had shown her how acute he was.

It was not easy to get away from people at Bryn Terfyn and to walk along the hillside to Ty Corniog. The last few weeks had shown her how hard it was to leave people just to be alone, and that was probably why she had begun to put her thoughts on paper, talking to herself without anybody listening. But that had its limitations. At times, when writing, she felt the need to expand, to go somewhere to find a living person of a different opinion, or indeed of no opinion. Her diary merely said amen to her own thoughts. It would be good to have an occasional talk with someone like Uncle Edward who knew nothing about the circumstances, nor about the relations between man and wife. The others all thought they knew something, and they thought and judged, seeing matters through the half open door of their knowledge.

At breakfast on Monday she said she would like to go to see Uncle Edward one day.

"I'll come with you," her sister said immediately. "I haven't been for some time."

"Do you go often?" asked Lora.

"No, not very often. Why do you want to see him now?"

Jane had not seen the sting in the word "often".

"Because I've come so near to him, and I'd like to walk on the hillside."

"He was every bit as near to you when you were in town, for the bus stops near his house." Lora blushed and took the point, but her neglect of him was merely part of her general withdrawal. Jane was sure to think

97

that she was after his money.

"I didn't have time to go visiting him or anybody else, and I'm sure he wouldn't want to see me often," said Lora.

"You had more time than I have."

"True enough, but it's silly to gad about when you might use the time to improve your mind by reading."

"It would have done you no harm to visit your own family."

"To quarrel with them? Uncle Edward had no use for Iolo."

"Then why do you want to go to see him now?"

"I want to get to know him better."

"There's not much to understand, he's just a miser and that's all."

"He isn't mean in some ways," said Owen. "He's bought a house that's much too big for him, and furnished it well."

"I'd like to see him, and that's all there is to it," said Lora. "I don't see why you can't do what you want sometimes, just because you want to, without always having to say why you do anything." She rose and went out. The children were playing in the field and she promised to watch them flying a kite.

"She's got her back up," said Jane. "I don't know what's come over Lora; she's as prickly as a hedgehog. You can't say a word but she flies off the handle."

"I marvel she's as good as she is," said Owen. "I don't know what we'd be like if we'd gone through what she has."

"She ought to have pulled herself together by now."

"Don't be so cruel! If she'd been able to it would have shown she didn't think much of Iolo."

"If he had died she'd have more to complain about."

"Not at all! She'd know where he was and how she felt about him then. She doesn't know where she stands now, poor soul."

"Oh well!" said Jane as she cleared the table.

* * *

If it had not been for the children, Lora thought when she reached the field, she would have regretted coming here. She had imagined that a spell in the country would have calmed her mind. But where there were people, there was always bickering. She tried to remember whether it had always been like this, but she couldn't. Hitherto, each visit to Bryn Terfyn had been innocently happy, no-one at cross purposes, going home after enjoying themselves... whatever that might mean. She tried to analyse the feeling of pleasure, and the only conclusion she could come to was this: that they were exactly the same on their return home as they were when they went there, except that three hours of life had gone by, that they had enjoyed good food, had talked without quarrelling, which seemed to show that, superfically at least, they liked each other. But Iolo's departure had the effect of making everything people said sound like a scritch on a slate, and she wished she could deaden her ears to the sound.

Jane's attitude towards her was just the same as when she was a child and Jane a young girl, always scolding her. So it was this morning just because Lora wanted to go alone to see her uncle. She had always wanted to go alone, as a child, to see a new-born calf, a piglet, in case someone else should see her joy in looking at them.

Her heart was not in kite-flying this morning, and each time she tried to fly it, down it came.

*   *   *

"You must let it go slowly," said Margiad. "Don't give it too much string to begin with."

"Neither the kite nor I are in the mood... it's just making fun of me." But the children did not take much notice. They all wanted to try, and it comforted Lora to see that Rhys joined in with them all.

Jane had made up her mind to go with Lora in spite of everything, making Lora feel like a child who is never allowed to go anywhere by herself. Ty Corniog was just a house on the mountain-side, on the same kind of land as Bryn Terfyn, but sideways on to a narrow lane leading to the bus route. On this there were several houses, so that it was not isolated. All round the house the freedom of the mountain, and a view stretching from the Rivals to Anglesey, plenty of room to stretch one's wings and breathe fresh air.

Uncle Edward was sitting by the fire in the kitchen, the place clean as a new pin although he did not expect them. He was surprised to see them, and Lora was astonished to find the place in such good order. He had just finished washing up after dinner, he said, and he would have made pancakes for them if he had known they were coming.

"I'll make some for you," said Lora.

"No you won't! Since you've come here, I'd rather talk with you. I'd have come down to thank you for washing my clothes but for the rheumatics."

"Is it bad?" asked Lora.

"Every now and then. I'm not much good at washing floors nowadays. There's a woman comes up here twice a week to do that."

"Couldn't she do your washing for you?" asked Jane.

"That's a matter between Lora and me. I'm particular about who washes my underclothes."

"I never heard of anyone so fussy," said Jane.

"Nothing wrong in that," said the old man. Lora was of the same mind, and reflected that this was precisely why she had wanted to come alone.

"Can I have a look upstairs?" she asked.

"You're welcome," he replied.

There again everything was spotlessly clean. Four sizeable bedrooms, partly furnished. Lora was delighted, and she found the two sitting rooms and the pantry equally tidy.

"You've got a wonderful house here," she said when she returned to the kitchen.

"You're welcome to come here to live," he said.

"Why should she, and give up a good job?" asked Jane.

"That's no business of yours," he said. "She could go to school just the same, the bus passes the side of the lane."

Lora made no comment, still turning things over in her mind. She had no idea her uncle had so good a house. Above all, she loved the wild expanse surrounding it, and a garden with nothing but potatoes and lettuce growing in it, a good clothes line on the mountainside, no trees except a thornbush in the garden. How she hated a wet autumn in the wooded gardens in town, wet clothes, slush underfoot. That was how it used to be long ago in Bryn Terfyn, but now she realised how fine all this bareness was, freedom to breathe, so different from the stuffy and gossipy streets of the town. People might gossip every bit as much here, but they would not be on top of you all the time. By now, her uncle's offer was not so intolerable, and the house could be made even nicer.

"You and the children could be by yourselves," he said. "Having a passage running the length of the house makes things easy. I'd have the kitchen and the parlour on this side, and you could have the pantry and the parlour on the other side, and we'd all eat together in the kitchen."

"You've got it all well planned," said Jane.

"I haven't planned anything," he answered angrily. "Just describing the house."

"What he's saying is that it's quite suitable for two families," said Lora.

"True enough," he said. "Jane thinks a man plans his life from the moment he's born. You and the children are welcome to come here to live, Lora."

"Thank you," was all she said.

"She'd be a fool to leave her nice house in town, with plenty of hot water and all that," said Jane.

"You mind your own business," he replied. "Nowadays people think that if they've got hot water and a bathroom, the millennium has come. The only day you really want a lot of boiling water is when you kill a pig, and we don't do that these days."

Lora had time to think over his suggestion as they walked back over the mountain, for Jane had little to say. "I can't think who'd like to live with that old man," was one of her comments, to which Lora replied, "There's one thing to be said for him: he's not a busybody."

XIV

The week, in many ways a happy one, was drawing to an end. Lora had had plenty of work to do, plenty of play and talk, helping Jane in the house and Owen outside. The hay was all in, but there was plenty of heather and bracken about the hedges, and she and Owen had raked it in while the children flew their kite. On Friday morning she and the children went up the mountain after breakfast to gather juniper berries, it being too early for blackberries and too late for bilberries. They worked long and hard to pick the small fruit, but by ten o'clock they had gathered a fair quantity and she promised to make them a tart for tea. Then upstairs to make the beds, and as the wind was favourable, she promised to go with the children into the fields beyond to play. When she got to the yard, Margiad and Rhys were waiting for her and telling her to hurry because the kite was flying high. Then they heard the postman's whistle at the gate, and she ran towards him and found he had a letter for her. She walked back slowly, reading it.

"Who's it from, Mam?" asked Rhys.

"From Mr Meurig," she replied without thinking. Her sister was on the doorstep, having heard the whistle.

"What does Mr Meurig want to write to you about?" she asked.

Lora blushed: she had just glanced through its contents.

"Nothing in particular."

"Has he any news of Iolo?"

"No, why?"

"I thought he'd be the first to know, being his boss."

"No, if there was any news his mother and sister would be the first to know."

"Why do you say that?"

"It happens that I've got to know them by now." It was obvious that her sister was only playing for time.

"Is it true that Mr Meurig is always calling?"

"Where?"

"At your house."

"He's got one of his own."

"You know very well what I mean. They say he's always in and out of your place."

"If coming in occasionally of an evening is what you mean, then it's true."

"You know what that means."

"No I don't, except that he's shown more sympathy than many others have done."

"Sympathy indeed! He's a widower and wants a wife."

"He can't marry me, can he?"

"He could take steps towards it."

"When you came to me you thought it would be a good idea if I went there as his housekeeper."

"That's quite different."

"I see! You thought it would be harder for people not to make love if they lived in the same house than if a man came in occasionally to visit three women."

Jane went inside in a huff, but not without having a last word.

"I'm sure he doesn't come to see the two others. He's had plenty of opportunity to see them before all this."

Rhys had gone off before this conversation began, and when he saw his mother following him to the field, he ran back to meet her. He could tell by her face that something was wrong.

"Come and sit with me for a moment behind this pile of bracken where nobody can see us." She put her arm round him as they sat down.

"What's the matter?" he asked.

She was so upset that she did what she would have condemned in others, unburdening herself to a child, but she managed to restrain herself from going too far.

"Auntie Jane has been unkind," she said.

"About Mr Meurig?"

"Yes," she answered, without enlarging upon the contents of the letter, which was merely a note to say the street seemed empty without her, and looking forward to her return. But it was enough for her to see what the writer had in mind, and she could not be angry with him for revealing it.

"Stay here, Rhys, and don't follow me. Tell them I've gone to the village."

"Why?"

"It doesn't matter. I'm going to see Uncle Edward, but I don't want anybody but you to know." Rhys thought that was better for her than going to the village: it might mean something.

She went from the yard to the mountain path and turned in the direction of the village, and on reaching the road went back towards the mountain and took the sheep track towards the path leading to her uncle's house. She regretted having said anything to Rhys, for it would only make him wonder what was in the letter.

Meanwhile, Jane and Owen were having a serious discussion, Jane in a fit of temper unloading herself of all her complaints against her sister, and saying vicious things about her. She never imagined her husband would turn upon her: to Jane, there was only one attitude to be taken, and it was that of nineteenth century religion. She was overwhelmed when Owen said, "You've been very cruel to her."

"In what way?"

"Don't you know what she's suffering?"

"She doesn't look as if she suffered at all."

"No, she has to put a face on it for the children's sake, and she finds it hard."

"How do you know?"

"People don't have to confide in me for me to know that. She showed it clearly enough the night she spoke about the stolen money. You must remember Lora's the soul of honesty."

"She didn't take the money."

"Of course not, but try and put yourself in her place, a woman deceived by her husband, the father of her children. Whatever happens to him now, this will be like a black curtain hung between him and the past."

"Suffering or not, she oughtn't to give people cause for talk."

"The fault lies with those who talk, not with her."

"She could prevent him coming there."

"It probably never occurred to her that he only came there for a chat."

"Well, there it is. She got her eyes opened this morning anyway."

"Yes, and very cruelly." It was the first time Owen had said anything so unkind to his wife.

When Lora reached Ty Corniog her uncle was putting a fork into a potato to see if it was boiled—he had his dinner about eleven o'clock—and when he saw Lora he looked astonished.

"What on earth's the matter with you?" he asked.

"I've come to say I may be coming here sooner than I thought."

"The sooner the better. What made you decide?"

"My sister Jane."

"She wasn't a bit keen on it the other day."

"It wasn't she who persuaded me."

"Sit down. Get your breath back and tell me what's going on."

"I happened to get a letter this morning from Mr Meurig and Jane heard me telling Rhys it was from him."

"Who, that solicitor?"

"Yes, Iolo's employer."

"Well, what of it?"

"Jane said rather pointedly that his purpose in calling wasn't what it seemed to be."

"*Does* he call to see you?"

"He drops in some evenings and the four of us have a game of cards."

"What concern is it of hers who comes to see you?"

"That's just what I say."

"People are just like that here with me, fussing about how much money I've got, how many sheep and ponies on the mountain. As soon as any of my ponies stray on to the road they're on to me, taking me to court and fining me. Let them mind their own business. Was Jane nasty?"

"Very."

"She can be. Owen's a much better type. Never mind them, come here to me."

"I'll see when I get back."

"Dry those potatoes, and get some buttermilk and some butter from the pantry and put them on the table."

As before, Lora found some solace in eating. The potatoes were white and floury, the butter and buttermilk excellent.

"Take plenty of butter," the old man said. "You could do with some more flesh on you. I've decided not to keep ponies on the mountain," he went on. "The two that are there can end their lives there instead of down a pit."

"It's cruel to send them there."

"No more cruel than killing lambs for Easter. Rhys—and what's the name of that girl of yours?"

"Derith."

"Where did you get such a silly name?"

"It's a Welsh name."

"Well, Rhys and her can play with them on the mountain."

"They'll be delighted."

Crossing the mountain on the way back to Bryn

Terfyn, Lora felt relieved at having had this talk and of the further evidence of how little her uncle cared about other people. Pity she herself could not be as little concerned! Perhaps you could not reach this plane of indifference unless something big occupied all your thoughts, just as her uncle was absorbed in his money making and could snap his fingers at all who criticised him. The cotton grass and the moss, the rocks and streams usually delighted her, but today, like many old friends, they had no message for her.

They had finished dinner at Bryn Terfyn, and Jane merely asked dryly if she wanted anything to eat. She just said no and went to make the tart for the children. A most unhappy tea time, although Owen and the children enjoyed the tart and ate heartily. Jane and Lora both looked miserable.

After tea Lora went to the field, making an excuse that she was going to play with the children. She sat down by the pile of bracken and looked at them, and her thoughts took a leap twenty years into the future. Something was bound to take the place of all this happiness; they would have moved into the unknown with no-one to direct their steps. But there was no need for the unknown to be as unstable for them as it had been for her.

Margiad left the others and came up to her. Rhys was the only one who turned to look at her, but he was so engrossed in play that he did not follow.

"What's worrying you, Auntie Lora?" she asked.

"Nothing much. Your mother and I don't understand each other properly."

"She's nasty with me too, sometimes."

"Is she?"

"I get scolded if I'm late coming back from the children's meeting or the school bus, or if I suggest going down to the village in the evening."

Lora remembered how fond Jane used to be of going to the village in the evening and racing back home.

"And she'd like to keep us here on the mountain Sunday and weekday and holiday."

"That would be a pity."

"But this week has been so happy, Auntie Lora," she said as she put her arm through hers.

"I'm sure it's done us all a lot of good, especially Rhys."

"Yes, he's a fine chap. I'll miss you very much."

"Would you like to come to us for a week, say next week?"

"Oh! that's just what I was going to ask you! Guto and Now are going to Llanberis to my father's brother, but I don't want to go there."

Owen came to join them and Margiad went to play with the other children.

"I never saw anything like Jane's behaviour this morning," he said as he sat by Lora's side. "Spoiling a nice week with all that silly narrowmindedness."

"Yes, she went a bit too far."

"I'm afraid I was very angry with her."

"I'm sorry, Owen, but I seem to cause unpleasantness wherever I go. Everybody's at cross purposes with me."

"That's not the way to look at things. It will do no harm to Jane to hear what she heard this morning. No-one could have a better wife, but I can't understand this fear of hers that someone should bring disgrace upon the family."

"Just as if our grandfathers had turned lots of people out of chapel because they sinned!"

"Exactly. But Jane isn't all that religious, you know. She just goes to chapel once on a Sunday and that's all."

"I'm afraid we're all like that nowadays. None of us has any experience of religion, or we'd understand other people's experiences better. A pagan of a miser like Uncle Edward is less of a busybody than anyone. I've almost made up my mind to go and live with him."

"His house is easy to divide," said Owen encouragingly. "You needn't be on top of each other."

"The town holds nothing but memories, and I'd like

to make a fresh start." Owen pricked up his ears at this: obviously there was no truth in the gossip, nor in Jane's accusations.

Before they left next morning, Jane had come to herself, enough at least to be friendly, to refuse to take any money and give them butter and potatoes to take home. The children were in tears at parting, Now and Guto going to the wall of the yard and sobbing away, then Rhys and Derith joining the chorus. Margiad tried to cheer them all by promising they would soon be together again. Even Lora broke down, the longing of the children releasing all her pent-up emotion.

There were some letters under the door when they reached home, one from her friend Linor in London saying she was coming to see her next week. This raised her spirits, but they soon fell. Perhaps she would have nothing to say that would calm her mind, and they might find themselves further apart, as had happened with so many of her friends. She thought of Mr Meurig's letter, but it only raised another problem by suggesting something more than mere friendship. She sat in the kitchen, listless, not wishing to do anything. At times like this in the meaningless moments after returning home, she rebelled against the harsh domination of living. Rhys came and sat on the arm of her chair.

"We had a good time, didn't we?"

"Yes, love, we did."

"Then why are you so sad?"

"It's always like this when you come back from holiday."

"Miss Owen comes back tonight."

"No, not till Monday she says in her letter. Auntie Linor is coming here next week."

"And so is Margiad, though we've just seen her."

"Never mind, it's a change for her."

"She's changed too, not so rough as she used to be." "Isn't she?"

"No, she's very kind to Guto and Now, though she does treat them as if they were still babies."

"They'll soon be too big for that. Suppose we get down to tidying up the house and we'll have salad and these potatoes for dinner."

"Shall I go and do the shopping now, and that will save you going this afternoon."

"Splendid!"

Something spurred her to action, preparing the meal and dusting everywhere so that by teatime everything was done and they enjoyed their bread and jam. What pleased her was that her heart had spring enough in it to help her to start again.

By evening she had nothing to do, for it was too late to start on any big job. The children were out playing, having taken up life where they left it, and she realised that this was the first time she had felt so lonely since Iolo was in the army. But then there were letters to expect and to answer, filling the vacuum in her life. She was sorry Loti Owen couldn't come back tonight—perhaps Mr Meurig might look in. She wanted to see him, and yet she didn't because of his letter yesterday. But for that, she would have welcomed his company.

Time dragged on her hands. She must get something tasty for supper, for the children anyway, and as she had plenty of eggs she went to the garden to get parsley and thyme for an omelette. Her next door neighbour came to the hedge.

"Did you enjoy yourself, Mrs Ffennig?" she asked.

"Yes indeed, plenty of fresh air, play and work."

"It will do you good."

Lora didn't answer, for she had nothing to say. Her neighbour had plenty to tell her, had she dared to.

"Have you enough thyme and things like that, Mrs Roberts?"

"I'd like some if you can spare it."

"You're welcome," said Lora. As she approached, Mrs Roberts saw how broken-hearted she looked.

"It's a pity you came back so soon, Mrs Ffennig. Another week would have done you the world of good."

"I don't know. Miss Owen comes back on Monday morning."

110

"She could look after herself."

"Yes, but somehow one wants to be home," she sighed.

"You must try to forget, Mrs Ffennig. You've got your own life to live." This was as close as she had ventured since that unforgettable morning in May.

"I do my best to forget, but somehow other things keep on drawing you deeper into your own hurt. It's not the event itself that hurts, but what comes in its wake."

Her neighbour had no idea what she was referring to, but said sympathetically, "Yes, I'm sure. Are you alone this evening?"

"Yes, until the children come in."

"Come in here for a moment."

Lora was happy to agree, finding Mrs Roberts's kitchen very comfortable, as comfortable as her own, but somehow different, which pleased her.

"Shall I make you a cup of tea, Mrs Ffennig?"

"No thanks. I've just had tea, and I'm getting things together for supper."

Her neighbour didn't know what to talk about without blurting out the fact that Iolo had been seen around during the week, and she did not know Mrs Ffennig well enough to feel able to tell her so startling a piece of news, so she said, "Rhys looks much better."

"Yes, he does. Better in other ways too, mixing well with other children. I was worried about him, always hanging around in the house, but he enjoyed every minute of the holiday with my sister's children in Bryn Terfyn."

Lora was on the point of telling her neighbour that she felt a longing to go to the country to live, but she said nothing in case the rumour got about, and she might change her mind. Finding Lora so friendly, Mrs Roberts nearly told her about Iolo, but for some unknown reason she did not.

As she left for her own house Lora said, "Thank you so much for this talk—you've no idea how good a turn you did me by inviting me in. There's something so depressing about coming home after being away." She felt that Mrs Roberts was not so distant as her neighbours thought.

The three of them enjoyed the omelette and dawdled over their supper. For once there was no need to hurry to do something else, and the children didn't want to go out to play: the days were shortening and it was almost dark before they finished.

"This time last night we were in Bryn Terfyn," said Rhys. Yes, thought Lora unhappily, thinking of that quarrel.

"Do you like playing the game 'this time yesterday, this time a week ago, a month ago'?" he asked.

"Yes, if it's something nice."

"What I liked was Gel," said Derith.

"Yes, he's a nice old dog."

"Now can do what he likes with him, but I was a bit afraid of him."

"He wasn't used to you. Would you like to go to live in the country?"

"Yes!" said the two of them eagerly. "But there isn't an empty house there," added Rhys.

"We could go to Uncle Edward's," said Lora.

"The man with a moustache?" asked Derith.

"And the mountain ponies. But he has no room for us," said Rhys.

"Yes he has—it's a big house and we wouldn't be in each other's way all the time."

"But we'd have to leave Miss Owen and Miss Lloyd behind."

"We won't think about that now. Let's think of something else. What about going over some verses for tomorrow?"

"You read them," said Rhys.

"All right—we'll do them together. What shall we start with?"

"The Lord is my shepherd," said Derith. They went through the psalm, Lora and Rhys glibly, Derith stumbling.

"What were you thinking about?" Lora asked suddenly.

"About that little stream in Bryn Terfyn," said Rhys immediately. "And you?" he added.

"About the sheepwalks near Ty Corniog. And you, Derith?"

"About tomorrow."

"Why?"

"Because I'll have to say these verses in front of a lot of people."

Although she took her time over washing the children and putting them to bed, it was still quite early. She waited for the ring of the door bell, opened the door, looked up and down the street. No-one about. Across the way, at Mr Meurig's, darkness. She went back to sit in the kitchen, tried to read and failed. No wish to write in her diary—she noticed that it was only when she was disturbed that she wrote, not when she was bored, as she was tonight. She began to think again about Mr Meurig's letter, and found it hard to reconcile with his absence tonight. It was not so much that she wanted to see him as to see anybody. She realised that she was not reconciled to her loneliness, and went to bed so as not to magnify it. She found herself thinking about that quarrel with her sister and rebelling against it. Why should she bother about what her sister or anyone else thought? She would have enjoyed Aleth Meurig's company tonight. Perhaps, after all, her quarrel with her sister had given her more pleasure than a quiet uneventful week would have done. There was some satisfaction in plumbing the depths of people's minds by quarrelling than by merely acquiring a superficial knowledge of them.

XV

Aleth Meurig found the week of Lora's absence the loneliest and emptiest he had known for many years, his house the emptier because the street was empty. He tried to convince himself that a week was not long, going to the Crown for an hour or so of an evening, talking to various people, and on returning home thinking over his feelings about Lora Ffennig. He realised that he longed more and more for her company, and that his liking for her was growing in a quiet way, without much passion. Quietness was part of her charm, like that of a secluded valley which you might miss if you passed through it by train or bus but which would grow on you if you lived there.

She had played little part in his life in the past, for he had not liked her husband and had no desire for his company after office hours. He found now that she was not easy to get to know, and to penetrate through that superficial coldness of hers he would have to see her often. He was always finding some new trait in her character: the night her sister-in-law had burst in on them he had thought her a fool, but had since changed his mind.

On Wednesday night, coming home from the Crown, he saw a tall figure crossing the street towards him. He recognised the walk. It was Iolo Ffennig.

"Hullo, Ffennig?" he said at once. "Who'd have thought of finding you here?"

"I've been looking for Lora." Meurig's surprise turned to alarm.

"She's not home—gone with the children to her sister's."

"When will she be back?"

"All I know is that Loti Owen doesn't return till Monday morning."

"What's *she* got to do with it?"

"She lives there now."

"I'd like a word with you, if I may "

"Come in for a minute."

Sitting down in the parlour, Iolo Ffennig began with,

"What I want to know is, what are the prospects of a divorce?"

"Yes... well..." said Meurig, much relieved.

"I understand you've been hanging round Lora," said Iolo.

"What do you mean by 'hanging round'? Of course I know what it means in common parlance, but what do *you* mean by it?"

"That you're after her."

"What does that mean?"

"Don't pretend you don't understand me. You know very well what I mean, that you've been making love to her."

"First I ever heard of it."

"Don't be so stupid. Everybody else knows."

"I'm sure they know much more than I do. If seeing a woman with three others a few evenings a week is making love, it's the strangest way of going about it *I've* ever heard."

"So you *do* go there."

"Yes, I do." He was about to explain when he realised that it would amount to apologising to a man he owed no apology of any kind. Looking at Iolo sitting there and questioning him so boldly, his temper rose, but he knew that anger would only bring harm on himself, and he recovered enough to go on.

"Yes," he said, "I like going there, but unfortunately I never see Mrs Ffennig alone. I did once, though, in the office. She was very worried and came to see me."

"Oh?"

"Do you want to know why?"

"No, I can guess."

115

"You spoke of a divorce. I suppose you thought you could get one because of her relations with me."

"Not entirely."

"The only way I can see is for Mrs Ffennig to seek a divorce from you for desertion, and she'd have to wait three years for that."

"I'd like to marry Mrs Amred immediately."

"Does she want to marry you?"

"We both want to get married."

"And you expect Mrs Ffennig to clear the way for your sake?"

"She could do, if—"

"Yes?"

"If she wanted to marry someone else."

"I see. I haven't the faintest idea what Mrs Ffennig intends to do, but I'd have thought getting married was about the very last thing."

"How do you know?"

"Don't think I'm in her confidence, nor is anyone else, but looking as if she'd been cut to bits is hardly a sign of wanting to get married, I'd have thought."

"She obviously doesn't expect me to come back."

"I wouldn't know about that."

"She's put new locks on the doors. I never thought she'd think of such a thing, being such an unsuspicious person."

"Perhaps events make us more suspicious."

Iolo got up to leave, and Meurig noticed that he was not so neat as usual. His collar was dirty, his suit was crumpled, and there was a sulky look on his face like that of a child who has not had his own way this time. He straightened up and said goodnight.

After he had gone Meurig was glad to lie on the sofa, all of a tremble, much disturbed by Iolo's visit. He was angry with himself for not thinking of all he might have said to him, for not being alert enough to refuse to ask him in. He was even surprised that he could have talked to him, for forgetting to bring up the question of his having taken his money. He could have kicked himself for letting his former clerk get the better of him. But that was what Iolo had always done, by his unconcern rather than by anything he had said.

He began to wonder what Iolo really intended tonight, what he was doing in town this week with his wife away. The more he thought about it, the more mysterious it became, until finally all the strands seemed to lead to one person—Esta Ffennig. Looking back he could see that Esta contrived to visit her sister-in-law when he was there. Wasn't it possible that she and her mother knew where Iolo was? That he had sent them his address? As to marrying Mrs Amred, he could well believe that Iolo would not have a moment's peace until she got her own way; there must be a divorce without waiting three years, and what could be more natural than to come and see how things were, to discover his former employer's feelings about Lora? Obviously, it would suit him best to get a divorce because of his wife's misconduct.

Perhaps Iolo thought his wife really wanted a divorce so as to marry Meurig, and that she would be willing to go away with him for her own sake and thus do him a favour. But surely Iolo knew his wife better than that! In the end, he could find no satisfactory explanation for his visit. The most likely was that Mrs Amred had sent him to see whether there were any possible grounds for a divorce, and that he obeyed although he knew the contrary.

The problem was what to do in the immediate future. Lora would probably return on Saturday night, and as Loti Owen was not coming until Monday morning, she and the children would be alone over the weekend. If he called on Saturday or Sunday evening, Esta Ffennig might be there, and Iolo would be sure to find out, if he were still in town, and thus prove him a liar. So far as he was concerned personally, he did not care, but it would not be fair to Mrs Ffennig, so he decided to go to Llandudno straight from the office on Saturday afternoon and stay there until Monday morning.

Then he began to think over the way her in-laws had treated Lora, without any vestige of sympathy. Not that it was any concern of his, nor did she seem to trouble much about it. However, he decided to write to tell her how much he missed her. How he wished he could take Esta Ffennig down a peg or two!

The opportunity came sooner than he expected. As he walked towards the station on Saturday he met her in the street. "I see your brother's in town," he said casually.

She blushed to the roots of her hair.

"How clever of him," he went on, "to choose a week when Mrs Ffennig was away!"

That was all, but it was enough to show that he knew Iolo had been staying with his mother and sister, and still might be.

On Monday morning he called Loti Owen into his room in the office.

"Would you do me a favour?" he asked.

"Willingly."

"I'd like you to act as postman for me, just once."

"Surely."

"Iolo Ffennig has been about while Mrs Ffennig was away."

"Good gracious!"

"If she knew, she wouldn't have had the chance to tell you in the few minutes you were there this morning. Do you want to go back during your dinner hour?"

"I'll be going there for my dinner every day till school begins."

"Good. Here's the message then. Ask her will she please come here to see me on business. I had a word with her husband on Wednesday night and I think she ought to know what it's about. I kept away all Saturday and Sunday in case her sister-in-law came there. It's most important I shouldn't see her alone there."

"I see."

"I didn't want to write to her—she might spend the morning wondering what was happening, and it wouldn't be fair to ask her to turn out on a Monday morning."

"If you'd posted the letter this morning she'd have got it by mid-day."

"I never thought of that."

But he had thought of it. Giving Loti the message would have put her on the trail, for she would certainly have seen Lora coming to the office.

"Do sit down, Mrs Ffennig," he said formally, and went on in a friendly manner, "Don't be alarmed—you'll hear why I asked you to come here instead of my coming to see you. You simply must know what has happened."

And so, she thought, it had nothing to do with his letter. He pondered awhile and then said, "Has anyone told you your husband has been in town?"

"No—has he?"

"Yes." All the colour was drained from her face: he thought she was going to faint and was on the point of ringing for a glass of water, but she recovered herself. As tactfully as he could, he explained what had taken place between him and Iolo on Wednesday night. Not exactly so, but with a different emphasis, making it clear that he thought it was Mrs Amred who wanted the marriage.

"Poor Iolo," was all she said.

"Why do you say that?"

"You've said you were sure it was Mrs Amred who wanted the marriage, and you'll remember telling me some time ago that Iolo was weak."

"Yes, I do."

"I'm sorry for any weakling who gets into the clutches of a woman like Mrs Amred."

"He went into it with his eyes open."

"No-one does. If I'd had my eyes open when I married Iolo, it isn't him I'd have married."

"He might have been all right then. Perhaps the weakness developed later."

"It was in him all the time, only I was too blind to see it. Fortunately I stayed blind until last May."

"Why fortunately?"

"I lived in a kind of paradise, even if it was a fool's paradise."

"That made the blow all the worse when it came."

119

"Yes, but it saved the children a lot of unhappiness."

"Hard to say what's best in the long run. But if I may say so, I think he was afraid of hurting you then."

"To hurt me more later on."

"Yes, he was out of your sight by then."

"True," she said slowly and thoughtfully. "That was Iolo's weakness, doing things behind people's backs."

"That's true of his sister, anyway." He then told her what he had said to Esta Ffennig and went on, "Forgive me if I've interfered too much but I thought it would be better for you to know whether he came to see you or to stay with his mother. I hope I didn't go too far."

"No, I'd rather know where I stand with people. That's what was wrong in the past, not knowing. Thank you for letting me know like this at first hand, instead of half-truths and half-lies dribble-drabble from someone else."

"I didn't call to see you, and asked you to come here, in case your sister-in-law called when I was with you. It wouldn't do, after what I told your husband. Not that I care tuppence myself, but I know you would."

"I would, and thank you for that and for everything." She went out, a stricken woman.

When she opened the door of her house she thought the lobby was too dark and sultry to breathe in, and wished that moment, playing Rhys's game, that she was back in Bryn Terfyn with the wind from the mountain blowing round her.

Sounds of children in the kitchen, and a warm smell from the stove in the back kitchen, the table laid for tea. Derith and Rhys busy getting it ready, bread and butter cut, kettle boiling and all done.

"There," said Rhys. "The slices aren't very thin, but I thought you'd be tired."

"That's lovely. I didn't expect this."

"I put the cups and saucers on the table," said Derith.

"Did you, dear?" said Lora, singing 'Up we go, come what may' just to keep back her tears.

"Are you happy, Mam?" asked Rhys.

"Yes, first time for years I've found tea ready."

"Did Mr Meurig have any important news?"

"No, nothing really." Rhys looked at her but did not notice anything.

"What if we went for a trip to Colwyn Bay before school begins?" she said suddenly.

"Oh yes," they both said.

"Right, we'll go."

That evening Loti asked if she could have supper in the kitchen with them, and when the children were in bed they began to talk. Loti's face was freckled: she had been the round of friends and relations, all kind enough, but she knew all the time that she wasn't really at home with any of them.

"I was glad to get back here," she said.

"But it's good for you to see old friends. It isn't good to be seeing the same faces all the time, unless you love them very much."

"Maybe."

"I've had some very disturbing news today." She did not know how much Loti knew already, for she had brought the message from Mr Meurig. However, someone was sure to tell her that Iolo had come back: it wasn't likely that Mr Meurig was the only one to have seen him.

"That's what Mr Meurig's message was all about," explained Lora. "My husband was back in town the other day. Maybe it was only to see his mother. I just don't know. Mr Meurig didn't want to come here to tell me in case Esta called. It's upset me very much, of course."

"Naturally."

"I expect you'll hear all kinds of stories, but Mr Meurig saw Iolo and knows why he came. To me, the important thing is that we know now his mother and sister know his whereabouts, and he's probably seen them."

"I do feel sorry for you."

"Strange he should come when I was away."

"You're right there."

"It looks as if he knew, but I may be wrong. It's hard

121

to believe they don't write to each other."

"Mrs Ffennig," said Loti, with sudden boldness, "could you bear to hear something unpleasant about your in-laws?"

"I think so, by now," said Lora ironically.

"I ask because I know from experience that one can still be sensitive about such matters, even when things have gone wrong. All I'm saying is that you don't need to worry about your sister-in-law. No-one here thinks anything of her, and as for you, you'll be thought all the more of when you're rid of her." Lora made no comment.

"Have I hurt you, Mrs Ffennig?"

"I've gone beyond being hurt, Loti. I was just thinking what a fool I've been."

"Are things as bad as that?"

"Yes, they are. But perhaps when I've plumbed the depths like this, I'll be able to climb to the surface again."

"Yes, I expect so."

"If your feelings are lukewarm, it's no help to anybody."

"You're much too kind to Miss Ffennig."

"Not really. I was trying to keep the table level, for Iolo's sake, but I don't think there'll be any more need for that." Loti heard a note of finality in her voice.

Blow after blow, from one hurt to another. When I put the new locks on the doors, I never thought Iolo would come back. It was a kind of far-seeing fear, thinking it might happen, but not believing it would. I thought how terrible it would be if he came back to the house he left of his own free will, without caring, walking in as if it were still his, into a house filled with pain for months. Although I dreaded it, I didn't think he would. Because of what I did, he found the door locked against him. But it's no use worrying about that, although he could make a great deal out of it in court. I might as well confess the truth, that I've had a bit of a shock, never thinking that Iolo would want to marry Mrs Amred. In

122

fact, my greatest fear was that Iolo would ask me to take him back, thus posing a real problem. I'm quite sure I wouldn't have him, and equally sure that his asking me would have fed my pride. Mr Meurig may be right in thinking that she is pressing him, but obviously he is not unwilling. I can't believe it possible that a man could be weak enough to marry a woman against his will. I know Iolo would just turn stubborn, so he must be half-willing, if not entirely so.

Mr Meurig knows her better than I do, and that she will not easily let go of him. It's by wishing to marry her that Iolo has hurt my pride, though at the moment I felt sincerely sorry. I was looking into the future, she having caught him, turned virago, leaving him no way to free himself except by doing what he did to me. No use saying "Serve him right" about someone who has meant so much to you. I wouldn't like him to be cruelly treated, though a little discomfort would do him no harm.

I feel quite differently about his sister: she is the villain of the piece because she has shown how she hates me. I wonder if she knows about his dishonesty, or does she still imagine he is honest, that he does have something against me and that his escape is a judgment upon me? It would do her good to know the truth, but why should I tell her? The weapon lies in my hands, but why use it? What good does it do to trample on an enemy and stand triumphant over him? There's nothing left for the victor. The knowledge still remains with me, something she is ignorant of. The victory is mine, and there can come nothing but distaste out of using it. Esta may now feel on top of the world—long may it last her—but she's treading on a swamp. As for me, I'm better off, for my eyes have been opened. I also have been on unsure ground for some time now. I can never forget the darkness that encompassed me when I came into the house this afternoon. What Providence put it in the children's mind to get tea ready for me? That's what saved me. From what? I ask myself. I don't know unless from the abyss of despair, and when you reach that, you are not

123

*responsible for your actions afterwards. You are too far
down to try to rise up. But after that tea and the talk
with Loti tonight, I feel I can still make something out
of life. Linor comes the day after tomorrow. If I really
know her, she will understand, but, after all, even one's
friends change.*

XVI

When Lora went with the children to the station to
meet Linor she felt very shabby in her old cotton frock,
compared with her friend who looked so spick and span
in her dark blue costume, with hat and gloves to match,
and nylon stockings. Linor Ellis was a young widow
whose husband had been killed in the fire service during the London blitz, and she was now senior mistress
in a school. She looked prosperous, her suitcase and
her handbag were both expensive. But after five minutes' talk the effect of the difference in dress had van-
ished and both were just as they used to be when they
were students in Bangor and hard up. This visit was
not exceptional, for she came to see Lora each summer
from her parents' home, but it was different this time,
and she was not surprised to find that her friend had
changed a great deal. Lora had written to tell her about
her troubles, including the theft of the money, told her
everything, as far as one can in a letter. What she had
been unable to convey was her attitude and her feelings
about it all.

Lora wished it could all be forgotten and not discussed, but that was out of the question because it was
uppermost in their minds for a while. What was important to Linor was how her friend felt, and to Lora,
how Linor would regard it all.

They were talking about this and that over their tea, mostly about old college friends.

"Do you remember Maggie Bifan?" asked Linor.

"Yes."

"I see her occasionally in London, at meetings of Welsh societies and the like, and it's from her that I get news of those who were in college with us—she's a walking encyclopedia, knowing what's happened to everybody."

"A strange hobby!"

"Yes—tragedy for most of them. She seems to have taken them all to heart, to mother them, and now they're scattered they're like children in exile, and it grieves her when they're unhappy."

"Here's one more to add to her list of tragedies."

"I think someone like her could write a novel, in two parts: the first about a group of happy young girls in college, the second about what happened to them later."

"The second part wouldn't be as happy as the first, I'm sure."

"Not surprising, after a war like this."

The back door opened and in came Esta Ffennig. Lora looked aghast—she never thought her sister-in-law would come again uninvited. Esta looked sulky, but her face brightened when she saw Linor.

"Will you have a cup of tea?" Lora asked.

"Yes," she answered drily.

Lora was silent, unable to join in the conversation. It was too much even for her placid nature, and her temper rose. Esta and Linor talked as if Lora were not there, Esta behaving as if she were in Linor's house. Linor made the mistake of asking Esta if she were still at the grammar school, for nothing gave her greater pleasure than to talk about the school and about Miss Immanuel. When Lora came back with more hot water she heard Esta asking Linor whether there was any chance of her getting a similar job in London.

"None whatever," Linor replied. "There are thousands like you in London, well educated, for so many authors and Members of Parliament want secretaries,

125

and the standards are very high."

The temptation was too much for Lora to resist.

"Why do you want to go to London when you've got such a good job here? Unless of course you want to be near Iolo."

Esta blushed, then frowned and made an excuse to leave.

"Linor, would you have believed it possible?"

"No, I can't think how anybody could come for a meal and ignore the hostess completely."

"That's the way she's treated me for months. This is the first time she's entered the house since I came back from Bryn Terfyn, and she wouldn't have come today if she hadn't known you were here."

"How could she know?"

"Derith is always popping over there."

"You gave her a knock-out blow then, and I was nasty too. I just made up all that bit about secretaries ... I don't know anything about them."

Lora then had a chance to tell her about Iolo's visit to Aberentryd and her talk with Mr Meurig, guardedly because the children were present. After supper, with the children in bed, they really got down to it.

"I've been thinking about that back door," said Linor. "You ought to lock it after tea."

"I might lock myself out, and besides, it would give Esta more grounds for thinking that Mr Meurig comes here."

"What does that matter? No-one in court would believe her if she hadn't actually seen anything. Besides, you don't want her when someone like me is here, do you? You've got to suspect people until you find them out."

"There's no end to that and it only makes you unhappy."

"Really, Lora, for an energetic person there's something very lethargic about you sometimes, letting things go instead of watching them. Pity you weren't more suspicious of Iolo."

"Would I be any the better for it?"

126

"You might have prevented it happening."

"No, I'd only have hurt myself, and I'd have been suspecting even when there was no justification for it."

"Perhaps. It's hard to say. No doubt you've been trying hard to find out why this business of fooling around with Mrs Amred ever came about."

"According to his family, it was because I was too engrossed in caring for the house and the children."

"It would have been wrong to neglect them."

"I thought the only way to keep the family together was to make the home comfortable. But Esta's one of those clever-clever ones who think otherwise, living as they do all on top of one another and imagining that's an intelligent way of living."

"Yes, but a woman can become a slave to a house."

"I didn't—in my spare time I read books, instead of going to gossip in cafes. But after the war I found that Iolo wasn't interested in anything, just scanning the surface of things."

"Blaming the war for everything, I suppose, like so many others."

"Not entirely, but he did say that after the war he had no use for chapel."

"Why?"

"Because they had been so ineffective in stopping the war and making a better world of it."

"The old old story, the old excuse. Everybody talking about society and not thinking of improving themselves as they used to long ago. I'm sure he blames the war for what he did, instead of examining his own conscience."

"I'm glad to hear you say that," said Lora, with a sigh.

"I think taking your money is worse than running away with a woman," said Linor. "That's a different kind of temptation. And there are always restless folk like Iolo—it doesn't take a war to make them. They can never find peace within themselves, and Mrs Amred must have satisfied something in his nature I agree, and I'm afraid he's a weakling.

"Women are bad, too, remember. Do you know what I think of affairs like this? That there are women who imagine they're in love with married men. They begin to pay attention to them, flatter them, and if the man ever complains about life at home, he unburdens himself on another woman. And what joy it is to an unmarried woman to have a husband telling her all the secrets of his home life! It isn't the man she loves, it's the sense of victory over his wife."

"There's a lot of truth in that. I never thought of it before."

"What kind of a woman is this Mrs Amred?"

"Neat and pretty at first sight, and even after. Hard as nails, and according to Mr Meurig, if she doesn't get what she wants, she'll get her revenge."

"Poor Iolo!"

"That's what I said, too."

"I'm sure it's she who is insisting on marriage."

"So Mr Meurig thinks. But Iolo can be very stubborn."

"Sure enough when he's no longer in love."

"Have another cup of tea?"

"Thanks." She smiled. "I said that just like Esta, didn't I? Tell me," she went on reflectively, "do you like Mr Meurig?"

"Very much. A fine man, so far as I can see, and Loti praises him as an employer."

"Do you think you could ever marry him?"

"What a question to ask! No, I don't think I could. If you marry, you've got to be so much in love with a man that you don't see any of his faults."

"Has he got any then?"

"I don't know, but I'm sure he must have. I'm not in love with him, though a lot of folk here think I am, so I hear."

"I'm sure they do. That's the worst of living among people who have all grown from the same roots. Their business is yours. They take care of you when you're in trouble, even when you're on the road to hell, as they see it. They're responsible for your morals. As for me, I've been uprooted, and no-one cares whether I lead a moral life or not."

"I don't know why people decide you're in love with a man if he comes across the street to your house."

"Because they're evil-minded, knowing their own weaknesses and thinking everybody's like them. But the great thing now is for you not to care. You can't help worrying. Walk about the town and hold your head up."

"I wish I could, but I think everybody's passing judgement on me."

"Nonsense. But don't talk about it any more. I've just had an idea—I'm going to take you to Llandudno or Colwyn Bay tomorrow. Is there anyone who can look after the children so that we can be by ourselves, as we used to be?"

Lora thought for a moment.

"What can I do? I promised to take the children to Colwyn Bay before the holidays end."

"We'll take them with us then. Come to think of it, they deserve a treat as much as you do, to be fair. Life's no picnic for them either."

"No it isn't."

"I'm sorry I suggested going without them."

"It would have been nice to be free, but there you are!"

Lora had a better night's sleep than she had had for a long time. Instead of writing in her diary, she went over their conversation and felt glad that there was someone under her roof who understood her.

In case she went to her grandmother's to carry tales, they said nothing to Derith until the last moment. They spent the afternoon sitting down while the children paddled. The beach was crowded, but in the midst of all those strangers they could talk or doze as they wished. The sound of the waves, the talk and the laughter of children, the sight of the sea, all blending together under the blue sky; their own talk was something apart, as if they were out of tune with all but each other.

Window-shopping on the way to tea, they saw a grey-blue autumn frock, three-quarter sleeved, plain, but well cut. As soon as he saw it Rhys cried, "Mam, that's a nice frock for you!"

"So it is," said Linor. "Just the very thing for her—we'll go in and see how much they want for it."

In they went straight away. Lora tried it on, and it fitted her. Linor paid for it and for a blouse for Derith and a sleeveless jumper for Rhys.

They were having tea in a crowded cafe and enjoying it, and when they finished Linor offered Lora a cigarette. Seeing her hesitate, Rhys said, "Have one and enjoy yourself."

"Yes indeed," said Linor. "Start showing you don't care." And she took it.

Loti Owen came to the kitchen after supper for a chat, and while Lora was upstairs, they washed up.

"Tell me, Miss Owen, what kind of a man is your employer?"

"As an employer, excellent, quite straight, a man of principle, and generous too."

"I'm sure you'll think it odd of me to come out with a question like that."

"Not at all—perhaps you're thinking of all the gossip because he comes here."

"Perhaps I am."

"There's nothing in it, I can assure you. He comes in sometimes after supper for a talk and a game of cards with the three of us. If there's any other reason for his coming, it's nobody's business."

"That's true."

"All the same, I hope this gossip doesn't turn out to be true."

"Why do you hope that?"

"For one thing—to be honest, I wouldn't like to lose such good lodgings. But of course that's a secondary matter. I don't think he'd make a good husband for Mrs Ffennig. A man can be as near as possible perfect, but somehow you can't love him. That's what I think about him, though I admit it's only instinct tells me so. He's

130

very active, quick in his ways, and I feel he'd be too lively for Mrs Ffennig. She's energetic enough, but I've noticed that she likes to be quiet at times and doesn't want to go making a parade of herself as so many women here do. Some of them would give a mint of money for her beauty. I'm sure Mr Meurig would want his wife to go about with him a lot: he likes acquiring nice things like furniture and pictures for his house. And what about the children? Don't forget, Mr Ffennig had his good points."

"Yes, but only up to a point."

Lora came downstairs and that ended the talk. After Loti had gone to her room, the two of them had little to say to each other. They kept their resolution not to go back to the matter of Iolo, and by now, Lora had no wish to: it seemed Linor had said the last word on that subject. There was nothing they could talk about as they did in the old days: the curtain that had come down on this topic had come down on many other matters. Strange how you could take delight in trivialities when all was well.

All good things come to an end too soon. Linor has gone, and after two days full of happiness, life is empty again. The two of us able to talk freely—there's nothing better than that, and it did me good to talk to her. The worst of a diary is that it cannot answer back, cannot contradict nor confirm. I wonder why I was happier discussing my troubles with Linor than with anyone else? Because she understood better, or because she agreed with me? Everybody else behaves as if they were afraid to hurt me when they say anything about him. Perhaps they do, but last night Linor said the one thing I wanted to hear when she asked why Iolo didn't examine his own conscience. Was it because Linor said I was right that I'm happier for her visit? I cannot say, but she taught me one thing, and that was not to care. I ought not to, even if I did something wrong, but I didn't, for that's what Iolo did.

Margiad comes tomorrow, and it will help to fill the

house and it will also be a change. Why do we want a change? It was what Iolo wanted. And yet change comes unnoticed. If Iolo and I had continued as we were, there would have been change—from one end of a plain to another, and they do differ although they appear the same. But the change that has come over my life now is like suddenly coming up to a mountain and trying to climb its slopes without looking back because the ascent is so difficult. Not that it's any use looking back: you can't carry the past into the future, it just stays there, and stay it must. I remember that when my mother died I found the bed immediately after they had removed the body with her pillow still dented where her head had rested, and I wanted to keep the pillow for ever just as it was merely to see the mark of the head that had meant so much to me. But to no purpose; the life had gone, and that alone might have brought about another change. Better to keep her in my memory than that dent in the pillow which would only have been a thing remembered. Soon, Iolo's departure will be merely a memory to me. Any event in family life is like throwing a stone into a lake; first a ripple, short of life, turning into waves, spreading and then vanishing. Quite soon people will have forgotten about my troubles, and I shall be no more than one of those contemptible women whose husband had left her, no-one remembering why.

Miss Lloyd will be back in a few days and we shall restart life as it was at the end of last term, everything as it was before. A lake disturbed by a storm, and then settled down after it had passed. That is how things will seem on the surface. I wonder if my mind will ever reach that state of calmness?

XVII

"Did you used to like boys long ago, Auntie Lora?" asked Margiad as they sat in the kitchen after supper the first night she came to stay.

"What on earth makes you ask that?"

"Because I'm very worried."

Lora was astonished. She had noticed a far-away look in her eyes ever since she came to the house, but did not think it anything out of the ordinary in a girl of her age.

"Don't worry, but I'd like to talk to someone about it, and I can't to mother."

Lora was even more concerned.

"I'm sure you'd no idea where I was going tonight."

"None at all."

"I went to look for Iorwerth."

"Who's he?"

"Iorwerth Richards from school. I'm mad on him— don't say anything till I finish—and I thought he was mad on me too."

"Yes?"

"I don't know how to tell you. He used to send notes to me in class asking to see me in the village after school, and I used to go."

"Where to?"

"Down to the chapel, and then we'd go for a walk and he'd go home."

"Is that all?"

"Yes, honestly, that's all. I know you think we used to go up the mountain and kiss and do silly things like that. But all I wanted was to look at him, listen to him talking and saying he liked me."

"How old are you, Margiad?"

"Thirteen and a half."

"You're much too young to be thinking about boys."

"I don't think about them, only about him." She began to cry.

"It's a miserable time when you're beginning to be a young woman, isn't it?"

"Yes, it is," said Lora. "Come here, my dear." She took her on her knee and as she put her arm round her supple body, she thought to herself that she was only just leaving childhood and deep in her first love, the way ahead unknown, and grown-ups cruel in their lack of understanding.

"Does your mother know about this?"

"No," she answered shyly. "I wouldn't tell her for all the world—she'd half-kill me."

"Yes but you see, she'd worry in case you got into trouble, and she's providing for your education, isn't she? You can understand, can't you?"

"Yes, I won't be a worry to anyone any more," she sobbed.

"There, that's enough. You tell me everything and I promise I won't tell your mother."

"It's like this—he promised to write to me in the holidays, but he didn't. That's why I wanted to come and stay with you. I went out tonight to try to see him, and there he was with another girl from my class, Dorothy Evans."

Lora let her go on crying until she had cried herself out, her sobbing raising an echo in Lora's heart.

"Now listen to me, Margiad. What kind of a boy is Iorwerth? Is he clever in class?"

"Yes, very."

"Does he work hard?"

"No, I don't think so—he seems to find everything easy."

"And he's a good talker?"

"Yes, and handsome."

"You like him very much?"

"Yes—well, I used to."

"You don't like anybody else?"

"No, nobody."

"And you haven't been kissing and doing silly things?"

"No indeed."

"And you're hurt because he was with Dorothy, aren't you?"

"Yes, because I didn't go with anyone else."

"I'm sure you wouldn't like me to say anything about Iorwerth, would you?"

"I don't mind what you say, Auntie Lora."

"I'm trying to put myself in your place, and this is how I see it. If Iorwerth has failed you, he isn't someone you can rely on, is he?"

"No."

"Just suppose you were seven years older and had been friends with Iorwerth for three years and then he'd gone about with someone else without telling you, it would have hurt you more, wouldn't it?"

"Yes, I think so."

"He'd have become so much a part of your life that it would be harder for you to think of anything or anybody else. Do you know the best thing for you to do now?"

"No, I don't."

"Grind away at your work in school—you do like it, don't you?"

"Yes, most of it, but I've neglected it since I got mad on Iorwerth."

"I'm sure you did—that's the difference between you and him. He's gone on with his work just the same."

"He doesn't have to do much swotting."

"Now, if you want to forget him, make up your mind you're going to do as well in the exams, if not better if you can."

Margiad smiled and said, "I promise, Auntie Lora."

"Just think how proud your father would be. Didn't you say he wasn't so well?"

"No, not nearly. I'll work better now and I won't be afraid of being found out either."

135

"No, it's terrible to be afraid of being caught."

"Yes, it is. Do you know what happened recently, Auntie Lora?"

"No. Tell me."

"Uncle Iolo's sister saw me with Iorwerth after school one afternoon—we were walking together, and next morning Miss Immanuel called me to her room."

"What did she want?"

"To ask me what I was doing out with him after school."

"What did you say?"

"I told her a thumping lie. I said I'd been to the chemist to get something for father—that was true enough—and that I'd been kept waiting for a long time there—that wasn't true—and I'd missed the bus and Iorwerth had passed by and seen me and tried to find a way of getting me home without waiting for the six o'clock bus. But I'd missed the bus on purpose."

"And she believed you?"

"Yes, what else could she do? But things will be much better now, and different, for I won't be on tenterhooks afraid of being caught."

The front door bell rang, and Mr Meurig came in. After a word with him, Margiad said she was going to bed.

"Goodnight, Auntie Lora, and thank you very much." The tears were running down her cheeks as Lora kissed her.

"There you are," said Lora. "I may peep into your room on my way to bed. Goodnight."

"Goodnight, Margiad," said Mr Meurig.

"Something has upset her, obviously," he said after she had gone.

"Yes, a great to-do. She's mad on a boy in school and has seen him with another girl."

"Poor soul!"

"I've been trying to put some sense in her."

"As if you could at that age!"

"She's promised to try, anyway. She's a good worker, and kind. She did a lot to help me today."

136

"Good for her."

"And she's got a good head on her."

"Pity she doesn't stick to her books."

"She's promised to."

All this helped to pass the time, and then there was an uncomfortable silence.

"I've just had a letter from your husband."

"What about?"

"The same thing. It's obvious that he's keen on divorce—or she is."

"Why does he write to you?"

"I've no idea. Hard to make out from the letter—one can only guess, except that he knows well enough that you could take the first steps, seeing that he's left you."

"As the two of them have lived in sin so long, I can't see why they can't go on doing so."

"You don't know Mrs Amred!"

"Well?"

"It's like this. If anything happened to Iolo now, it's you who'd get a pension and anything he had to leave, and I know her well enough to be sure she's determined to get anything a wife is entitled to."

"I see. But why write to you?"

"He knows it would be easier for me to start you on that track than anyone else, and perhaps, in view of all the gossip about my coming here and things like that, he thinks I'd help for my own advantage."

"I see," said Lora, blushing.

"To tell the truth, I'd rather see him write to you. It puts me in a very awkward position." Silence again.

"I don't know whether I can dare to explain," he said boldly. "I'd like to see you get a divorce for my sake." Lora bent her head as he continued, "But urging you to do that I'd be helping your husband, or rather Mrs Amred, and I really don't want to do that. There's no knowing what use they'd make of it if I showed too much keenness. It works both ways: I don't want to help either of them, but I do want to be of some help to myself. All the same, I keep on telling you that you ought to get some financial help for yourself and the children. Just think what Mrs Amred is getting out of him."

She ignored that last remark, and started off in another direction.

"Remember that I'm not against him having a divorce just for revenge. That would do no good to either of us."

Such feelings were of no interest to Meurig.

"May I ask you a question, Mrs Ffennig?"

"Ask what you like."

"Do you still believe he'll come back to you?"

"There are no grounds for thinking so if he keeps on asking for a divorce."

"He or Mrs Amred. I'll put it this way. If he asked to come back do you think you'd let him?"

"Not now," she replied unhesitatingly.

"You weren't so sure a few weeks ago, were you?"

"No, I wasn't."

"May I ask why you've changed your mind?"

"Certainly. Other things have happened since then that make me refuse to think of it."

"Things he has done?"

"He and his family. He came here when I was away, and I am quite sure now that he knew I was away. That finished me."

Aleth Meurig felt that this was a step forward, though it was merely a negation.

"Thank you for your letter to Bryn Terfyn," she said.

"I couldn't help it—the street was like a cemetery. I missed you very much. Did you enjoy yourself?"

"Yes and no. It was a change to get up to the mountains and have so much fresh air and sunshine. But before I left, Jane and I quarrelled."

"No!"

She told him what had happened about the letter.

"If I'd known that, I wouldn't have written."

"Don't worry. I think the row will do her good, and Owen gave her a good scolding. She's narrow as a knife, though she isn't a bit religious."

"Isn't it strange how narrow-mindedness persists in the blood."

"I think that's half the trouble with this little girl. Her mother's at her all the time if she's late coming home and that kind of thing."

"What happened afterwards?"

"Things were strained but got better before I left. Fortunately my London friend came here this week, and she's shown me better than anyone what moderation means."

"I thought you looked happier tonight."

Aleth Meurig went home a little more optimistic about Lora's feelings. True, so far they were negative, but better that than some sentimental idea that she could take her husband back and such foolishness.

Margiad was reading when Lora took her up a cup of milk to her room.

"Drink this."

"Thanks very much, Auntie Lora."

"Can't you sleep?"

"No, I'm reading just to keep awake so as to have a word with you. I want to thank you for being so kind to me, but I couldn't do that while Mr Meurig was there."

"Feeling better now?"

"Much—I can see I was silly, and I'm ashamed of it."

"You're just like any other girl of your age. Every one of them thinks it's only her who's been naughty. Try and forget it."

"I'm going to work really hard."

"I'm going to take you to the hairdresser's tomorrow to get your hair cut."

"What will mother say?"

"I don't mean cut it short, just trim it at the ends where it's so untidy—it will grow thicker then."

"Auntie Lora, you won't tell mother anything about this, will you?"

"Not likely, unless someone else tells her. When did Esta see you?"

"A month ago, before we broke up."

"I don't suppose she'll hear anything, Go to sleep now. Goodnight."

"Goodnight, Auntie Lora."

On Sunday morning they all went to chapel, Lora in her new outfit. Margiad's hair had been cut, and plaited neatly down her back. Margiad felt as if she were going to chapel with the Queen and tried to walk accordingly. As they came out of chapel, she was aware that Iorwerth was standing there with a group of boys, but she did not look at him, walking erect and proud of being with her aunt.

XVIII

Annie Lloyd had been back for two days, and Lora in school for a week. Rhys had started at the grammar school and everything was back in the old routine, the days shortening and a fire quite welcome. Lora had not seen anyone from Bryn Terfyn lately, nor had she heard a word. She thought she ought to go there to see how Owen was, and would do so if she could be sure that Jane was in a more reasonable frame of mind. She knew she ought to go in any case, but she was tired of doing things that were difficult, so delayed it day after day until Miss Lloyd told her one afternoon that she thought her brother-in-law was very ill: she had seen Margiad looking very downcast, and heard someone say in the common room that the girl's father was very poorly. Lora asked Rhys, but he had only caught a glimpse of her since going to the grammar school, so Lora decided to go and see for herself.

It was somewhat colder than when she went there

in August, the wind blowing through her clothes as she took the mountain path from the road. She could see the children on the wall by the door looking towards her, then running to the gate. The wind drove them to shelter under the wall, by the gatepost, and it was there that Lora found them, like three hens sheltering from the wind and looking as miserable as hens do in bad weather, and every bit as shy.

"Father's very ill."

Lora was alarmed. "Why didn't you send word by Rhys, Margiad?"

"Mother warned me not to, so as not to upset you, and he's not so bad as Now said."

"That's good news." They walked in a row towards the house. Jane's head could be seen by the door post waiting for them. Lora was the first to speak.

"How's Owen?"

"So-so. The doctor sent him to rest in bed for some months. What he needs is rest and good food, he says, and then the other thing will recede."

Lora knew that the 'other thing' was tuberculosis. They sat by the fire, the children hanging round, Jane staring into the fire and rubbing her knee. Margiad's books were on the table, and Jane made no effort to prepare tea.

"You mustn't worry too much," said Lora.

"Easily said."

"Yes," sighed Lora as she got up and went upstairs. Margiad went back to her books.

Owen's face had changed since August: by now it was putty-coloured, with a line of white skin just below his hair. Beads of sweat were running down his temples. He held Lora's hand in his own hard-skinned one, his eyes shining.

"I'm glad you've come, Lora."

"I didn't know till last night that you weren't so well."

"I didn't want you to come here only to see me. I wanted you to come because I've been worrying about that quarrel."

"No need for you to worry about that. I'd have come some time anyway, and sooner if I'd known you were in bed."

"I know that, but Jane wouldn't let Margiad tell Rhys in school."

"I've been very upset since I was here last."

"Something new?"

"Yes. Apparently Iolo has been about while I was here and went to see Mr Meurig. He wants a divorce, it seems."

"That's for you to decide, isn't it?"

"Yes, of course, but Mr Meurig thinks it's Mrs Amred who is pressing him so that they can get married. I'm sure they don't like going on as they are."

"By now they don't, though they didn't care when they went off."

"People have to be respectable when they cool down."

"What are you going to do?"

"I don't know yet. If they're determined to get married, I'm the only one who stands in their way, and it would be silly of me to take revenge that way. But if it costs a lot, I can't afford it."

"Unless they promise to pay."

"You can't rely on their promises. What riles me is that Esta writes to him."

"Does she?"

"She must do. I'm sure he stayed with his mother and sister when he was in town, and how else could he have timed his visit when I was away?"

"Makes you feel you're living in a snake-pit."

"Yes, and what's worse they give people the impression that all the fault is on my side."

"Evil folk always do."

"But don't tell Jane about this last business, she always gets things muddled up in her mind."

"Yes," said Owen drily. "Before I forget, thank you about Margiad—she enjoyed herself immensely."

"She's a dear girl, and a good worker."

"Yes, she helps Jane a lot these days."

Jane came up with a tray, and Margiad with a

smaller one for her father. Jane looked more cheerful.

"What do you think of him?" she asked Lora.

"That he ought to take a long rest and eat as much as he can."

"I still enjoy my food," said Owen.

"Good. Is the milk from your cows all right?"

"So the inspector says—it's been tested."

"Drink as much of it as you can."

"That's what I told him, Auntie Lora," said Margiad.

"Margiad has taken to drinking milk since she was with you," her mother said. "And thank you for having her."

Margiad looked meaningly at her aunt.

"Thanks for coming," said Owen as Lora turned to leave. "Come again soon."

"I will."

"But you've got plenty to do too," said Jane kindly.

"Yes, but fortunately Mrs Jones who comes in to clean is quite good, and the two young women give very little trouble."

"Thank you for being able to forget," said Owen to her, as the others were going downstairs.

"We'll come to take you to the bus," said Guto, when she followed them.

"Right."

"And come back soon," said Jane.

"I might come on Saturday."

"Good."

"What did you think of father?" asked Guto, in a grown-up way.

"Better than I feared."

"Do you think he'll recover?" asked Now.

"Sure to, so long as he's content to stay in bed and eat enough."

"I'm working hard now," said Margiad.

"So I heard."

"Who from?"

"Your father."

"I don't mean helping mother, but in school."

"That's fine."

"I may be going to school in town next year," said Guto.

"Will you?"

"I hope so."

"When are you coming back, Auntie Lora?"

"I'll try to come on Saturday."

"When can Guto and I come to stay with you like Margiad?"

"There's no room now."

"We'll sleep on the floor."

"We'll see, we'll manage somehow. Goodbye."

While Lora was at Bryn Terfyn, Loti and Annie had been sitting in their room, Loti trying to study, Annie just meditating.

"You seem very bothered," said Loti, looking at her friend.

Annie stared at her as if she were a stranger.

"You've been like that all through the term," said Loti. "Is anything worrying you?"

"Yes, I feel really unhappy." Loti put down her book. "Yes, I'm absolutely fed up."

"With whom?"

"Everybody, I think."

"Strange to hear you say that. Am I too much for you?"

"Not a bit, not more than anyone else. I'm sick of the school and of this town. Nothing seems to stay the same, ever."

"It doesn't—it's just that we expect it to. I realised at the beginning of the term that this was the eighth time I'd be giving the same lessons to the lower forms. I've been here seven years."

"Nothing wrong in that."

"No, but what will it be like in ten years?"

"You'll be married before then."

"No sign of it yet. And that Esta—I could murder her."

"Lord above!"

"It may be my fault, knowing too much about her brother, and seeing her always hanging round the

144

headmistress. If I'm late in class, Esta is sure to come out of the head's room, and I'll bet you she tells her. I can't go on living in dread like this."

"It's harder for Mrs Ffennig. There's no doubt Esta knows where her brother is, and that she knew Mrs Ffennig would be away when he came here."

"Poor Mrs Ffennig."

"Esta watches everything that happens here, and tells her brother how often Mr Meurig comes."

"What's the matter with the woman?"

"I'd say that she can't face up to the fact of her brother's dishonesty. She'd like someone else to be guilty."

"I wonder if she knows about the office money."

"I shouldn't think so."

"Pity she doesn't—that would cramp her style."

Derith put her head in and said, "Rhys is sick."

"Where?"

"In the kitchen."

They both rushed in and saw him vomiting. Annie went to get some cold water while Loti held his head.

"Better now?" asked Loti.

"Yes thanks."

She went to get a bucket and floorcloth to clean up the mess, and Annie put Rhys to lie in the chair and put a cushion under his head, and kept an eye on him. At that moment Esta came in through the back door.

"What's up?" she asked.

"Rhys has been sick."

"And his mother gadding about somewhere!"

Annie was furious. "If she is, she's doing it on her own money, anyway!"

"What do you mean?"

"Go and ask people who know."

Annie went into the parlour and Loti said to Esta, "She's gone to Bryn Terfyn because she heard last night that her brother-in-law was very ill."

"And so, obviously, is her child," said Esta.

"Rhys was all right when she left, weren't you, Rhys?"

145

"Yes, but Aunt Esta blames mother for everything," he said, hanging down his head.

Soon they heard the front door opening and in came Lora.

"What's the matter?" she asked.

"Rhys has been sick, Mrs Ffennig."

"What did you have for dinner in school?"

"Stewed beef, stewed plums, and custard made from custard powder."

"I thought so. You'd better go to bed."

Lora could sense the awkwardness caused by Esta's attitude, standing there with a sullen look. Lora felt as uncomfortable as if she had been responsible for it all. The look on Esta's face gave her strength enough to lift Rhys and carry him upstairs like a baby. Esta left, and Loti went to the parlour.

"I've put my foot in it now," said Annie.

"Best thing you could do. She might come to her senses if she knew a few things."

"I got so angry when she talked of her gadding about that I couldn't help it. But I must explain to Mrs Ffennig." When she heard Lora come down she went to the kitchen and told her everything.

"Don't worry, Miss Lloyd," said Lora. "It's done and that's that. No, she didn't know about it, not from me, anyway. It may do no harm. You can't help these things. I'm more worried about Rhys."

"Really? I'm sorry."

"He's been complaining about a pain in the stomach for some time now, but this is the first time he's vomited. I must get the doctor to take a look at him."

Lora sat by the fire a long time, just thinking. She gave Derith her supper and put her to bed. On her way down she looked in on Rhys, who was still awake, his head aching. She sat by his side and put her hand on his forehead.

"How cool your hand is!" he said. They sat for some time in silence.

"How was Uncle Owen?" he asked.

"Rather poorly, but not so bad as I feared. He'll have

146

to rest in bed for a long time."

"Pity, isn't it?"

"Yes, but he's sure to get well. Do you think you can go to sleep now?"

"Yes, I feel better, but I haven't done my homework."

"Never mind that. I'll explain to the school—you go to sleep and you'll be all right by the morning."

Lora was almost too worried to tell Mr Meurig all this when he came in later.

"Look, Mrs Ffennig, there's no sense in going on like this. You work like a slave and keep on worrying while other people enjoy themselves."

"Let them. I don't want their money," she said, and then added, "But I'll have to try and have dinner at home."

"More work for you."

"No, if I pay Mrs Jones a little more she'll prepare dinner for us all—she cooks her own as it is, and it will only mean an extra half-hour for her."

"You know best. You're afraid your sister-in-law may have heard about the money, aren't you?"

"Yes, but it couldn't be helped."

"It may do her good. Those people she mixes with at that art society brag about their broadmindedness about sex and such matters, but stealing money would be something quite different."

"Maybe. But isn't it strange, it never rains but it pours."

"Everything's on top of you now, but a change will come."

"I wonder!"

"You go to bed now," he said.

He went home, and Loti Owen came in to say that Annie wouldn't be having her usual cup of tea tonight. "She's in such a state, worrying herself to death," Loti said.

"Tell her not to worry so far as I'm concerned," said Lora. "She may have done me a service in the long run."

Lora learnt more about the affair after Loti had told

her of the discussion between the two of them before Rhys fell ill.

Rhys was asleep when Lora looked in on him on her way to bed. She noticed how his face had changed in the last few months, lengthening, his head that of a much older boy. She must go to see the doctor in the morning, and wished she did not have to wait till then. She was too wide awake to sleep, so she took up her diary.

My troubles are growing, and now of a different nature—illness. Any other time I'd have worried about what Esta said and did, but Rhys put all that aside. The boy is fretting, and not getting the right kind of food. I can't get the faces of the Bryn Terfyn children out of my mind, they're even clearer than Owen's. How sad they looked tonight! Come to think of it, they've never seen illness at Bryn Terfyn. Jane saw plenty before she married, but the children have seen nothing worse than flu. And they are so cut off from the world up there on the mountain. I don't suppose they see other children once they've left school. Bryn Terfyn, their parents, the cows and pigs, the cat and the dog, that's their universe, and so their father's illness is something very real for them. They were so glad to see me, and unlike their mother, eager to show it. What small-minded folk we all are—my delaying my visit to Bryn Terfyn although I had heard that Owen was worse, and Jane today so cold and distant. And yet I'm sure she was glad to see me, or she wouldn't have asked me to come again soon.

Isn't it strange how reluctant we are to show the best side of our nature to each other? When we quarrel, we can pour out our worst feeling freely and give vent to all our hatreds. Perhaps we are sorry afterwards. But we hardly ever release our good feelings, quietly or out loud, and if we did we feel sorry and ashamed—indeed we feel ashamed of them before we express them. Why could I not admit to myself tonight, looking at Rhys, that I loved him from the bottom of my heart? I was afraid of doing so.

Pity we can't always look at people as if we were seeing them for the last time. But there's some silly pride inside us that keeps us stiff-necked, afraid of bending, as if we'd lose something extraordinary by doing so. "I won't do this, I won't do that" and always the emphasis on "I". I'm just the same with my mother-in-law, and she with me. How easily we can persuade ourselves that this affair is altogether different.

But I pity the children more than their parents. Poor Margiad! But her father's illness may take her mind off that other business, and she's young enough to be able to stand pain. If her father is ill for a long time, or if he dies, she'll be expected to sacrifice a great deal.

What is the matter with Miss Lloyd? A quiet girl like her must have been greatly stirred to give battle to Esta, but then I know nothing about what happens in school. I want to hold on to this monotonous life, and she wants to change it. I was the same at her age. How I have changed! It no longer hurts me when people say unkind things about Iolo, whereas a few months back it hurt me to the quick. I hope Rhys recovers, and Owen too. I feel imprisoned in this house and would like to get away.

XIX

Things settled down again, Rhys better, the doctor saying it was due to nothing much more than eating something that did not agree with him. Owen was holding his own, even getting a little stronger, his doctor confident he would recover without going to hospital. Obviously, things were a bit tight at Bryn Terfyn, but

149

Lora did not hear her sister complain. Lora herself was happy in school, her old school. Some of the staff who were there when she married were still there and it was handy for her to leave Derith in the infants' school and to take her home. The work was not too heavy, but it did mean that she had to concentrate. They all came home for dinner except Miss Lloyd, and Mrs Jones came for five mornings each week. However, there was plenty for Lora to do at night—ironing, mending, preparing tomorrow's dinner as far as possible, and also going through her work for school. She soon found that there was little money left by the end of the month.

She decided to keep Saturday afternoons free for taking the children out, for they had nothing but the street and the playing field to play in, and that did not give them much scope. She no longer took them with her to Bryn Terfyn. Her sister's children came down occasionally on Saturday afternoons, and only an unexpected day off kept her from being completely exhausted. Miss Lloyd seemed to have recovered her morale and went about as cheerfully as she used to. Loti Owen worked hard of an evening, and this gave her room mate more freedom. Aleth Meurig called as usual, but as the days shortened he came earlier and generally found Lora alone. Ever since that letter she had received in Bryn Terfyn she could see the purpose of his visits and tried to avoid thinking of it, putting it at the back of her mind, and yet knowing quite well that it could not stay there unless he changed or went elsewhere.

She wished she could have a long spell away somewhere, longer than she had ever had, to find out what she felt about him, and also to discover what his feelings were. But there was no chance of it, and she could see herself slipping into the same state of stagnation that was characteristic of her married life, talking to her friends in the kitchen, one of them with a purpose other than mere conversation. She also realised that even in her diary she was being evasive, turning it into something like the evening talks in the kitchen, insincere, a literary exercise, a mere frill, instead of revealing her true feelings, her fears concerning Aleth Meurig. She felt that by not telling him to keep away she was tempting him to come. If he stayed away, she would lose much that quickened her dull life. She felt that she could not help being inconsistent and unfair simply because she was too listless and weak to be otherwise. That was exactly how it had been with Iolo, letting him have his own way without a word to stop him. It was not for the sake of peace that she kept silent, merely letting things slide because it saved trouble. It was also less trouble to do the housework than not to, for to let things go at home would cause all kinds of difficulties. Doing it made life smoother, though some people thought keeping a house tidy was easy enough.

Thoughts of this kind rose up from the very depths of her consciousness and made her blush, but she put few of them into her diary. It was on one of these nights, after thinking a little about her future, not profoundly, only as much as her listlessness allowed her, that Aleth Meurig called and found her by the fire darning stockings. For a while he watched her working away without lifting her head.

"Mrs Ffennig, you're not going to go on like this?"

She looked up.

"Like what?" she asked, unable to conceal the fact that she understood what he meant.

"You know very well what I mean. You surely don't intend to go on working away like this until you're sixty?"

"No, I don't—the children will be earning then, and there'll be less to do."

"That's twelve or fifteen years ahead."

"What else can I do?"

"I've suggested that you should get a maintenance allowance, but you won't hear of it."

"No, I won't."

"Do you think you could marry me if you got a divorce?"

Lora looked down and busied herself with her darning.

"Could you?" he asked again.

"I'm afraid I couldn't, and it really is too sudden a question to try to answer like this."

"Would you like to think it over?"

"I'm afraid the answer would still be the same."

"You don't really know me very well, do you?"

"You never know anyone until you marry them, and not always then. Time doesn't seem to have anything to do with it, somehow."

"No," he said thoughtfully as he lit a cigarette. "It's a matter of taking a blind chance."

"Yes. You only do that once—at least I do—and I did that with Iolo. I don't think I could do it again."

"Are you sure?"

"I am at the moment. If I was really in love with you, you wouldn't have to come here to ask me. I'd have met you half-way somewhere and we'd have decided to get married."

"But there *is* another way of being married, you know, perhaps the only way for you and me."

"Maybe. But we'd have to do it with our eyes open."

"Well, what's stopping us?"

"Nothing so far as you're concerned, but I've got the children."

"I don't see that as a hindrance."

"Not today, perhaps, but you might some day. It would be too late then."

"They're no different from other children, are they?"

"Not so far as I know, but if they knew I loved someone else they might change."

"That wouldn't be too hard to deal with."

"Maybe not, if I was sure it was they who meant most to me or you."

"I see," he said, turning round in his chair. "Well,

let's leave things as they are tonight, shall we? I wonder if Miss Lloyd and Miss Owen would join us in a game of cards before I go." It was the only solution to the problem of how to leave without saying any more on the subject.

* * *

"I've had enough—let's make this the last game," said Lora.

"So have I," said Loti.

"Just one more," said Meurig.

"Yes," said Annie Lloyd.

But another game was more than Lora could bear.

"For heaven's sake let's have a talk over a cup of tea," she said. "I can't stand all this card-playing in complete silence."

Loti went to help her with the tea.

"Well, what shall we talk about?" asked Aleth Meurig. "There's nothing for us to discuss, and that's why cards are useful. Four of us sitting here with nothing in common."

"We all live in the same street," said Lora.

"We've all had the same kind of education," said Annie.

"And not one .of us is interested in anything but work," said Lora.

"In that case we're very different from most people today," said Meurig.

"Don't talk to me about work," said Annie. "I'm not interested in it."

"Why not?" he asked.

"I'm getting fed up."

"With work?"

"No, with doing the same thing year after year."

"You ought to get married," he said.

"That would mean work, too."

"Of a different kind. You wouldn't get fed up with

153

working for your husband." They all saw that the conversation was moving into a dangerous channel.

"I believe you've got to have some incentive to carry on," said Loti, and they all agreed. "But the incentive must come from within you, not from outside."

"That's meant for me!" said Annie.

"For us all. I felt that at the beginning of summer. We all keep on waiting for some external event, just to give us a change. And that change drives us on until we get used to it, and then we wait for something else to happen."

"In other words," said Meurig, "if you want to marry, you've got to try it without waiting for the incentive to come to either of you." Lora turned her head towards the fire.

"What do you think, Miss Lloyd?" he asked.

"Depends whether you're a man or a woman," she replied.

"It makes no difference nowadays," he said.

"Why must we always talk about marriage?" asked Loti.

Lora agreed with her, but showed no inclination to say any more. She had plenty to say on the subject of incentive, but not here, not in a discussion that lacked sincerity, not between four people. She felt as uncomfortable as she used to be in chapel at her old home when listening to people relating their spiritual experiences. She was sure then that they were made up for the occasion, just like tonight's talk in the kitchen, talking just to prove how penetrating they were. They all condemned Esta and her set for talking over their coffee in cafes, and here they were, doing exactly the same.

"I propose we end this discussion," said Lora.

"Who wanted to start it?" he asked.

"It wasn't altogether spontaneous, was it?"

"No, we just talked for the sake of talking," said Miss Lloyd. "If we'd really started revealing our true thoughts, the kitchen would be emptied in a flash."

154

"That would be for two of us to decide," he said.

"Or for one," said Lora sharply.

* * *

When he got home that night, Aleth Meurig pondered long over this conversation. It was of course insincere, but there was truth in it. Who would have thought of Loti Owen except as a hard-working woman, and Annie Lloyd too, by all accounts. She also was dissatisfied. Of the three of them, Lora Ffennig was the most difficult to get to know. She was at the same time warm-hearted, and yet cold and distant. Could it be true that Iolo had grounds for complaining about her devotion to the children, and were the children themselves a problem? He was right in thinking that an overriding devotion made her forget everything else. Was he himself in love with her? When she was away, he thought he was. But it was quite clear by now that he could not persuade her to divorce her husband, nor to go away with him so that Iolo could divorce her. How quickly this could be arranged in England or France! He found Lora Ffennig condemning her sister for being so narrow-minded, but she herself was little better. The three of them here tonight seemed to be without any joy in life because duty came first. So they would continue, and at the end of their dull lives, someone would say over their graves, "What they could do, they did." True about Loti Owen and Mrs Ffennig, at least. Miss Lloyd's attitude of rebellion against her work seemed a healthier sign.

In bed, Lora went through all the happenings of the night, thinking of all she might have said, but did not. Aleth Meurig had disturbed her so much that she could only wait for her mind to settle down and see things more clearly. Too great an upset to write about, too personal. It was not something just to put down in a diary, but something to be faced up to. She was glad he did not pursue the other subject when they were all together, although Loti had spoken her mind and said

155

that there must be some incentive from within. She would describe it as faith in life, and what was important was not to let external matters extinguish it when the flame was low. But she couldn't for the world have said that before the others. Could she have dared to, to someone else? She didn't think so, unless he was out of sight.

XX

The problem of the children rose in an unexpected way, and yet, when the headmistress of the infants' school sent word to the other school to ask Mrs Ffennig to come to see her at the end of the afternoon, the first thing that came to her mind was that Derith had done something wrong. It never occurred to her that she could have anything good to say about the child. She had long ceased to expect that from any quarter.

"Sit down, Mrs Ffennig," the headmistress said, coming to the point at once. "It's very unpleasant, but I must tell you because you are best able to deal with it. It's hard for me to have to tell you, but we've caught Derith stealing." This was the last thing Lora expected to hear.

"Stealing?"

"Yes, but wait a minute—it isn't the ordinary kind of case. I don't think we've ever had anything like it before. I don't know how to explain properly."

Lora had strength enough to ask, "What has she been stealing?"

"Mostly the children's sweets. Some of them kept on complaining that they were losing their sweets from their pockets in the cloakroom, or from their desks. And sometimes pieces of bread and butter."

"She had no need of either—she gets money for

sweets, and bread and butter to eat at playtime."

"Yes, but what's strange is that she didn't eat any of them. I tried to find out by asking the children to own up, but no-one did, and I had to search in their desks and even in their pockets. I found one child's sweets in Derith's pockets. The child was able to describe them accurately and how many there were of them—you know how children count everything. And Derith didn't deny it."

"I'm very sorry," said Lora. "But I just can't understand, for obviously she didn't want them."

"Neither her teacher nor I can understand it, in spite of all our questioning. All she did was to laugh in our faces. I told her how wrong it was, and still she smiled, so we thought the best thing was to let you know, Mrs Ffennig."

"Thank you, Miss Huws—I'll do my best, though I think she'll be just the same with me. She's a difficult child to understand."

"That's how we see her too."

"I'm sorry she's given you and her teacher so much trouble."

"Don't worry—it's part of our job, and things like that get worse nowadays."

Lora went to look for Derith, but there was no sign of her, and she had to go home without her. She overtook her at the end of their street, walking head down and kicking dead leaves off the pavement.

"Hullo Derith, you've got ahead of me today."

Derith just walked on, head down.

"Give me your hand." But she snatched it away.

"What's the matter with you?" No reply.

"Come on let's hurry and you can help me get tea ready for Miss Lloyd and Miss Owen. We're going to have fish today."

"Are we going to have chips as well?"

"Yes, if there's enough time."

Derith gave her hand at last, but without raising her head.

Lora lit the fire in the parlour and poked the kitchen

fire, and began to get tea ready.

"Look Derith, come in the back kitchen and you can have a piece of cake." She went willingly.

"You've been in trouble in school today, haven't you?"

"Yes," she said, head down.

"Now dear, I'm not going to scold you until I know why you did it. You've been taking other children's sweets and bread and butter, haven't you?"

"Yes," she replied quietly.

"But you didn't want them, did you?"

"No."

"Well, why did you do it? Tell your mother—perhaps you may be ill."

Derith lifted her head and replied, "No, I'm not ill. I did it for fun, to make fun of the teachers."

"That's not the way to have fun, and it's very wrong to make fun of people."

"It's her fault."

"Who's she?"

"Miss Oli, our teacher."

"Miss Oli? Is that what you call her?"

"Yes."

"What had she done to you?"

"She's an old bitch."

"Where did you learn that word?"

"We all say it."

"About whom?"

"About Miss Oli."

"Is she unkind to you?"

"Yes, she shouts at us and pinches us on the sly."

"But why did you steal the other children's things?"

"Just for the fun of seeing her look for them and not finding them."

Lora took her hand and went with her to the kitchen, taking her on her knee before the fire.

"Derith, you've been a very naughty girl." She looked her mother in the eye and smiled.

"Teacher had been unkind to you, hadn't she?"

"Not just to me. To all of us."

"Had the children been unkind to you?"

"Oh no!"

"Not even those whose sweets you took?"

"No."

"Tell me now, if someone had taken your sweets, what would you do?"

"I'd feel hurt."

"The others felt hurt, too, and it was your fault."

"But I wanted to make fun of Miss Oli."

"Well, you didn't. She made fun of you. And the children won't like you now and won't play with you." Derith began to cry.

"You can see how silly you were, how naughty. Would you like to be friends with the children again?"

"Yes."

"Do you know how? By never doing it again. Will you promise me you'll never steal again?"

"Yes."

"I won't punish you this time. Do you know what else you've done? You've hurt your mother very much." Derith began to cry again, and Lora was not sorry to see it. At other times, when scolded for some misdeed she had run out, showing no signs of caring, but now she sat sobbing by the fire. When Rhys came in through the back kitchen his mother gave him a sign not to speak to Derith.

Lora decided not to stay indoors that night to talk to anybody. This life of work and idle chatter made her feel like a discarded boot on the common, left there for years. After putting Derith to bed—she had recovered by then—she put on a warm coat and went down to the quay to try to clear her mind. It was a typical late September evening, a touch of mist that made her turn up her coat collar.

She sat on the wall of the quay, staring idly at the water. It was good to be doing something useless, if only just looking. The light from the houses nearby ran smoothly over the water, waves lapping against the wall, the vague figures of couples moving along the quay. It was on such an autumn night that she and

Iolo decided to get married. The memory did not move her as it had for many years after they married. The decision in itself was important, fateful, different from anything else in life except death, and as much of a leap into the unknown as that. The difference lay in its being her own choice, this forward leap. The ecstasy remained unchanged from that night until the war.

Her mind turned towards her latest concern about Derith. She was not so despondent as she feared—was it because she was getting accustomed to trouble? Sense enough in the child's reasoning, if you could believe her. That was the point: if you could believe her. The very crux of the matter. She seemed to be sorry when she went to bed, putting both arms round her neck, something she had not done for a long time. But she didn't pursue that line of thought any further. The quiet lapping of the waves and the distant lights drew her into dreamland.

The flickering lights on the water, changing every moment, brought her to a state of lethargy where neither work nor thought mattered. That was all that had been her lot for six months, that and a few hours' sleep at night. She had come to believe that neither hand nor mind could ever be idle again, as if she had to keep on knitting so that time could pass by without her knowing she was alive. Occasionally she heard quiet laughter from a young couple sitting on a bench opposite, and she remembered W. J. Gruffydd's poem about the yew tree in Llanddeiniolen churchyard ... "their turn will come." Not too soon, she hoped, whoever they might be. She sat there a long time, listless in body and mind.

Soon, she saw a figure approaching and recognised her walk. It was Esta, and to avoid her was impossible.

"Hullo," said Esta.

"Hullo."

"I've been to your place and they told me you'd gone for a walk, and I came here to look for you."

"And disappointed to find me alone for once," thought Lora.

Esta looked different tonight, that sullen look had gone; she seemed downcast, much plainer than usual. She had turned up her coat collar and fastened it with a pin, although there was a buttonhole.

"Don't you feel cold here?" asked Esta.

"No, it's better than being at home—it's always so stuffy indoors." Lora tried to guess why she had come to the quay to look for her.

"I've had more bad news today," said Lora.

"Oh?" said Esta drily.

"You'll know about it soon enough, for it will be all over the town. Derith has been caught stealing at school."

"Oh?" said Esta, most unsympathetically. "Stealing what?"

"Other children's sweets and bread and butter. But she didn't eat them."

"What did she do with them?"

"Just kept them."

"What for?"

"To make fun of the teachers searching for them, she says, out of spite because the teachers were unkind."

"I've heard that Derith's teacher is unkind—wouldn't it be better to take her to another school?"

"No, if it's in her that wouldn't stop it. We'll see what happens."

Esta did not reply immediately, but then said, "Mother and I have been upset by what Miss Lloyd said the other night."

"Perhaps she ought not to have said it, but something had upset her too."

"I think she ought to stand by what she said, and prove it in a court of law."

"The less you have to do with lawyers the better, Esta, you'll only burn your fingers."

"What do you mean?"

"Just think—I'm sure you have some idea how much your brother earned," (she found herself saying your brother, and not Iolo) "and that he couldn't afford to

161

spend money on luxuries for Mrs Amred and keep his family on his salary."

Esta made no comment as they walked along, and as they parted, Lora asked, "Won't you come in?"

"No thanks."

Rhys was sitting by the fire in the kitchen, and Lora could see that he had not been doing much work.

"Where have you been?" he asked. "Mr Meurig called."

"I went for a breath of fresh air—there's been some trouble about Derith in school."

"I thought something had happened." When he heard the story, Rhys began to cry.

"Don't cry—I don't think she's a thief, for she didn't keep any of the things for herself, but just to spite the teacher."

"I hope that's true."

"I'm going to write to Linor and ask what she thinks."

"Yes, do."

"Remember, Rhys, don't let Derith think you know anything's happened. That's the best way of stopping her doing it again. I think I've taught her a lesson, and she's very young."

"She doesn't look as if she cared."

"Don't think any more about it. How much more homework have you to do?"

"Not much—nothing for tomorrow. Aunt Esta looked in."

"Yes, I saw her on the quay."

"Had she got as far as that?"

"Yes, she had. We'll go to bed early, and try not to worry."

"It would be nice to go somewhere else to live, wouldn't it?"

"Yes—we may go to Uncle Edward's—we'd be welcome there."

*I feel totally different tonight after this latest blow—
I never thought it possible. I feel stronger, better able to*

162

fight. I was nearly prostrated when I first heard the news, but after hearing Derith's account I felt I could defend her, and that her teachers did not understand her. It was their attitude, not their words, that gave me that impression. Perhaps I'm like my mother-in-law, fighting for my children through thick and thin. She's a difficult child to understand, as slippery as an eel— sometimes I think she's not all there, with that meaningless smile on her face, but she's learning well in school. That's why I was glad she cried, though she's capable of putting it on as an act. She was brought up at a difficult time, when I was too concerned about Iolo to take enough interest in the children. Rhys was older, and had found himself by then.

I think now that I ought to have said more than I did to Esta. When I'm not with her, I feel bold enough to tell her all I have in mind, but in her presence I'm cowardly. I expect she thought she would find me out with Aleth Meurig tonight. She has no sense of humour. And what a chance she missed to hit back at me when I spoke of getting mixed up with lawyers! Anyone with a spark of wit would have said I ought to know something about them. I don't see why she and her mother should be kept wrapped up in cotton wool against hurt. They are utterly selfish people. I feel better after saying that, and not having to talk to anybody tonight before going to bed. Derith is fast asleep.

XXI

Lora decided to go to Bryn Terfyn the next day after school, and to go there alone. When she told Loti Owen at dinner time, Loti suggested she should go by the school bus and so have more time there. She would make tea for everybody if the children could wait until she came home from the office. Rhys could give them a snack to wait.

Owen was still in bed, looking much the same, and Jane looked rather poorly. Money must be getting short there by now. Watching Jane cutting bread and butter, she thought of Uncle Edward nearby with all his money, more willing to take from Jane than to give. For tea there was nothing but bread and butter and jam, both home made, it was true, but she wondered if they had something more nourishing for supper. Margiad was growing fast and getting thinner, even little Now was not such a lump of a boy as he used to be.

"Do you like eggs?" Lora asked.

"Yes," they all said and Jane added, "They're scarce now that the hens are moulting, otherwise we'd have them for tea every day. What there is we keep for Owen. Why do you ask?"

"Only that I thought Margiad was growing too fast and ought to eat lots of eggs."

"She has as much milk as she likes, and so do the others."

"I eat a lot of cheese," said Now.

"Good for you!" said Lora.

Lora was afraid that her sister was economising on some things so as to be able to buy others, but she knew she would be furious if she suggested they ought to eat plenty of nourishing food. She wondered whether to suggest that Margiad should come to her house for dinner every day, for in school she would only get the same dinner as Rhys.

"I'm always hungry after school dinner," Margiad said.

"I'd like you to come and have dinner with us," said Lora.

"You've got as many as you can do with as it is," said Jane.

"One more doesn't make much difference. What do you say, Margiad?"

"I'd like it very much, but you've already got a lot on your shoulders."

"We've a bit to spare for the cat every day."

"Thank you very much, Auntie Lora."

"Uncle Edward came here yesterday. Now don't throw a fit—he gave me a pound!"

Lora suddenly put her cup down on the saucer. "What's come over him?"

"Finding he's near his end, I'm afraid. He looks worse, and more frightened of being alone in the house."

"He ought to have someone there with him."

"Why don't you go, Auntie Lora?" asked Guto.

"Yes," said Margiad. "We'd see much more of you then."

"It wouldn't be a bad idea. Rhys said last night he'd like to live in the country."

"There's one thing to be said for it," said Jane. "You wouldn't be much bothered by him and his ways, for the house is convenient enough, and could be made quite nice. There's an outhouse full of nothing but firewood and odds and ends, and it could easily be made into a wash house."

"What kind of lighting has he?"

"An oil lamp, as you might guess, but they've brought the electricity to the two houses at the end of the road where the bus stops, and it could easily be brought into the house."

"It would be hard to persuade him to do that."

"I don't know—he finds it hard to fetch the oil."

"He'd send Rhys for it."

"You never know—you try. I don't think it's so hard to get him to part with money by now."

Owen knocked on the bedroom floor.

"What do you want?" asked Jane from the foot of the stairs.

"Just hearing you enjoying yourselves talking away, and I'm out of it." Lora went up to him.

"We were talking about Uncle Edward."

Owen smiled. "Did Jane tell you about his parting with some of his money?"

"A pound—he could easily have made it five."

"A pound is a lot for him. If it was only half a crown,

it would show he's beginning to loosen his purse-strings. You never know what may come out of it next."

"I've been thinking seriously of going to live there with him. I'd like to make a fresh start—I'm tired of town, and Rhys said last night he'd like to live in the country."

"I'd be delighted, Lora. From here to Ty Corniog is no distance for us country folk. It would be fine. I don't see enough people."

"Don't you?"

"No. You know how it used to be in the quarry, fun and laughter every day. Fair play, they still come here, but I'd like to have more company and there's only you and Jane left of the old family now."

"Yes," she said thoughtfully. "Strange, isn't it, and we're so young."

"We'll get some fun out of life yet," he said hopefully. "Something tells me every day that I've got a long life ahead of me if I make the effort."

"What's hard is to get the incentive to try."

"Yes, but you find it in your own family, Jane is kind, and so are the children. Think of Uncle Edward— he'll never find that incentive."

"It's his own fault."

"Yes, hoarding money is a strange hobby."

"It will be no use to him in his old age."

"But you can't help feeling sorry for him, can you? And he did say he'd be glad if you went there to live."

"He knows who's a fool and who isn't. Isn't it strange," she went on, "that the ass who's used to a heavy load keeps on carrying it?"

"Yes, but you mustn't call him an ass. Call him a fool if you like, but there are fools and silly fools." He laughed and began to cough.

Lora thought Owen had a long way to go to recover, judging by the hollows behind his ears and his thin neck. She would have liked to stay to keep him company and enjoy a longer talk. It was hard to leave him, the long night ahead of him, tomorrow like today, the fine weather ending, mist over mountain and sea. Yes, the attempt to recover demanded an incentive.

"You've a nice view from this window," she said.

"I never look through it now—I did at first, but I've begun to live with my thoughts."

"And with Williams Parry," said she, taking his poem 'Summer' lying on the table by his bed.

"I find comfort in it—it tells you what is in your own mind."

He turned his head towards her with a look of longing in his face as she went through the door. "Come again soon."

"I certainly will," she replied.

The children took her to the road, and Guto asked her again, "How did you find him, Auntie Lora?"

"A good deal better," she replied.

"The doctor says he is holding his own."

"He'll recover, you'll find."

"When can we come to you?" Now asked.

"I haven't forgotten about it—there'll be an empty bed when Miss Lloyd goes away at half-term."

"It's cold," said Margiad, shivering.

"Haven't you got your winter clothes on?"

"Not yet. They want mending and we've been too busy."

She gave them a shilling each, and in the bus she thought she ought to buy some wool to knit for Margiad.

When she got home, Rhys was alone in the kitchen. He looked pale, and didn't seem to have done his homework.

"Are you ill?" she asked.

"No," he replied unconvincingly.

"What's the matter then?"

"Nothing much."

"There's something wrong."

"Only the children playing in the street tonight."

"Stopping you doing your work?"

"No, not that."

"Were they doing something wrong?"

"Just playing a game about a man running off with a woman."

"What does that matter?"

"One of the boys caught hold of Derith in his arms and ran away with her shouting 'I've caught Mrs Amred'."

"You could see them through the parlour window?"

"Yes, and Derith came in crying, and when they saw me they ran off."

"When did Derith go to bed?"

"Immediately after."

"Never mind, don't take any notice of it and try to laugh."

"You never laugh."

"No, it's wrong of me."

"Why?"

"Because I've been worrying needlessly."

"You couldn't help it."

"Perhaps not, but things might be worse. What if I was like Uncle Owen?"

"Is he very ill?"

"Not very, but he'll have to stay in bed for some months, and they might be short of money. We're healthy at any rate, and I've got my salary."

"Margiad is getting very thin."

"Yes, I've told her she can come here to dinner every day."

Rhys winced.

"What is it?"

"I've got a pain."

"In your stomach?"

"Yes, it's always there."

"You can stay in bed tomorrow morning and I'll get the doctor. Go to bed now, and I'll bring you a cup of Benger's." Seeing him bend over brought a lump to her throat, remembering the day after Iolo left when the boy was doubled up in his chair. She sat by his side after he had eaten.

"There, that's better now. The faintness has gone," he said.

"How long have you had this pain?"

"A long time."

"How long is that?"

"Soon after Dad left."

"And you never told me!"

"It wasn't there all the time, just now and then, and it wasn't bad."

"We'll see when the doctor comes. Try to sleep now."

"I feel fine—I'm much better."

She went to the attic to see Derith and found her with the light on, hugging her doll.

"What's the matter, Derith?"

"Nothing."

"Aren't you going to sleep?"

Derith began to cry. "Nasty children!"

"Never mind them—we'll go away from them."

"Far away?"

"Yes, very far. Would you like a cup of Benger's?"

"Yes please—can I have it here?" pointing to the bedside.

"Yes, you'd better have it here, Rhys is ill."

Derith didn't say anything, and Lora could not make out whether she was thinking it over or just did not care about her brother.

When she went down the second time, someone had opened the door for Aleth Meurig, and he was standing in the kitchen, back to the fire.

"Hullo! You're quite a stranger—I haven't seen you for ages," he said.

She did not want to see him then, and did not feel at ease with him after his last visit.

"No, I've been out the last few nights."

He looked surprised, as if she had no right to go out at all.

"It's very quiet everywhere," he said.

"Yes, the children are in bed. Rhys isn't at all well, and I'm going to send for the doctor tomorrow."

"I'll telephone him in the morning."

"No, I'd rather you didn't, if you don't mind."

"Dear me, you're a strange woman. Miss Owen can do it."

She said nothing, but noticed the touch of mockery in his voice.

"You're worrying."

"Naturally, over one's own child." It was her turn now.

"How long has he been complaining?"

"He had one attack previously that I didn't know anything about, but he said tonight he'd had the pain ever since his father left."

"Does he vomit?"

"Not now, but he did the other night."

"You don't feel like talking, do you? Perhaps I'd better go."

"No, please stay, I'd be glad of company." It stung him to hear her say that instead of 'your company'.

"How was your brother-in-law?"

"Holding his own, but it will be a long business, and I don't know how they'll manage on the insurance money."

"And you're worrying—you'll be the next to fall ill."

"It's hard not to worry. After all, the last six months have been no holiday."

"No, I know, but worrying about other people won't help you," he said kindly.

"It takes the worry from one thing to another and takes my mind away from myself."

"That can't help you to forget, and it would take a complete change in your life to do that. Each time I see you walking down the street I say to myself that a woman as beautiful as you ought to enjoy herself in other towns, other countries, so that the world could see you, instead of being cooped up in a place like this."

"What good would that do me? The eye is never satiated with seeing."

"Come to that, what's the good of anything?"

"You get more satisfaction by staying where you are. I'll never know anything about the things I've never had. If I went travelling, I'd only be dissatisfied and longing to get home again."

"Yes, but you have to leave home to want to get back to it. And *that's* not a phrase I can claim copyright of either."

"I don't know. I think of singers and actors and people like that who at their best have had a world reputation, many of them ending their lives in sadness, nobody remembering their days of greatness. Besides, you can't turn an ordinary Welsh woman into someone like the grand folk in England."

"Forgive me for troubling you, but couldn't you think of something less than that, marrying me so that we could travel a bit? You wouldn't have to work so hard, and you'd have someone to stand by you. We can probably prove that Ffennig and Mrs Amred are living together and you could bring an action for divorce against him. But the simplest way would be for you to come away with me for a weekend so that he could sue you."

She shook her head, not daring to look him in the face. "No, I'm afraid I couldn't."

"You couldn't face the disgrace?"

"Could you?"

"I could for your sake, but it's obvious you couldn't for mine."

"I tried to make myself clear the other night. It would take something overwhelmingly powerful to make me seek a divorce."

"And you don't feel that way about me?"

"I'm afraid not. If I did, we wouldn't be arguing about it in front of the fire tonight—it would have happened without discussing it."

He lit a cigarette and stared into the fire.

"Do you realise you'd give Ffennig his freedom to marry Mrs Amred if you got a divorce?"

"What do you mean?"

"I thought you'd like to give your husband that amount of happiness."

"You mean that I'd sacrifice myself to let a man I once loved have his wish?"

"If you like to put it that way."

"I'm afraid I couldn't do that either. As you can see, I always put myself first."

"I didn't mean to suggest that."

"It may well be true. Disappointment does many things to you—it's made me see more clearly, made me wiser. And no wise person ever takes many risks."

He laughed cynically. "I don't know why I laughed," he said. "I'm feeling very downhearted. I'd get a lot of pleasure out of making you happy."

"I don't think I'll ever get that kind of happiness again, because of what's happened to me. I'd be on the look out all the time, and living in fear."

"That of course is something I couldn't understand."

"Try to forget me."

He said nothing, nor did he show signs of leaving. So Lora went to get supper ready. Still he did not go. It was a joy to see her moving about, so skilfully and deftly getting supper ready, and all stimulating to the appetite. For a moment he transplanted her in imagination to his own house, but she did not seem to fit in there as she did in a house full of school bags and toys in corners. He should have come first, not Iolo Ffennig, spending the years between now and old age with her.

"You're not making supper just for me?" he said.

"No, I must have something to eat—I haven't had a bite since tea at Bryn Terfyn."

"No-one else coming?"

"No, Miss Owen kindly made tea for everybody between five and six, but I'll take them a cup into the parlour."

"This is just heavenly," he said as he sat down. She felt so too, but did not say so. She was sorry for him, and at the moment felt kindly disposed towards him, no longer the solicitor, but a nice man enjoying his food, just as she had seen one of her brothers at his last meal before going back to France in the First World War—and with the same kind of longing in his eyes.

"How I wish this could go on for ever," he said.

"Other things will happen."

"Life is hard."

"So I thought in Bryn Terfyn tonight."

"Trouble of a different kind."

"Maybe, but it could leave its mark on the children."

"I doubt it—they soon forget."

As he went out, he shook hands with her, but said nothing.

"I'm sorry," she said.

"Goodbye," he said. "I'll be at hand if you're in any difficulty."

She went back to the fire, looking at the table with his knife and fork on his plate. There seemed to be some finality about it all, probably their last meal together.

She heard Miss Lloyd and Miss Owen going up to bed. Miss Owen looked in and said goodnight, but Miss Lloyd did not. On her way up she found Rhys sleeping peacefully when she opened the door, his face pale, dark lines under his eyes. She was anxious to know what the doctor would say tomorrow.

Of all the complexities of tonight's events, one thing only stands out, and that is Owen's brave and kindly face. It has left a deeper impression on me than the sad look on Aleth Meurig's face as he left tonight. Owen's face, Rhys's back as he got into bed. It's now that I realise what Iolo's departure has meant to Rhys. I don't suppose I shall ever know the extent of his suffering, whether it was the loss of his father or the suffering it brought upon me. And here I am, on so eventful a night, compelled to make up my mind about something really important. But perhaps it is not so important after all. We put too much emphasis on whether people marry or not. It would probably worry me more if other things hadn't happened. What if Owen were well and everybody in Bryn Terfyn happy? Or if Rhys didn't care whether his father had gone?

Here I am, isolated on an island, nothing else to worry about except that I'm alone, no-one caring about me. Isn't that exactly what would make me heedless, putting me in the mood to take a chance and accepting Aleth Meurig, thinking I loved him? How right Linor was in saying that love is often a fiction of the imagination! Was it something else that made me refuse him? I like him well enough, and I'm no longer in love with Iolo, not in the way I used to be. But could there be some trace of love for Iolo in my subconscious that keeps me back and prevents me from falling in love with Aleth?

I don't know. But I keep on seeing Owen and Rhys suf-
fering, and the sad innocent faces of the Bryn Terfyn
children. I'm sorry I made such a fuss about their food
tonight, but at least I found they weren't short of nour-
ishing food. Margiad shivering in the cold tonight—how
cruel we grown-ups can be to children! I wonder if Iolo
thought of that. Surely not, any more than I would if
I decided to marry Aleth Meurig. And that so clever
discussion tonight between us when I spoke my mind—
how different, how natural, the talk at Bryn Terfyn. But
I must go to sleep. I wonder why Miss Lloyd did not
come to say goodnight. And what of tomorrow? I hope
there's nothing wrong with Rhys. I must go and have
another look at him.

XXII

Aleth Meurig went back to his house, switched on the
electric fire in his front sitting room and sat in his easy
chair, slowly and automatically taking a cigarette out
of the packet, just staring into the fire. He had gone
across tonight hoping Lora would accept him, for his
mind had been full of her for weeks. He could not say
exactly when this began unless it was that morning
she came to his office insisting on knowing about the
money. Before then he only thought of her as his clerk's
wife, a handsome woman who greeted him politely but
distantly each time he saw her. But that morning, in
her suffering, she had revealed something of her character. Not that he liked her very much then; she was
so obstinate and insistent. He saw her as a woman who
persisted in knowing where she stood, and that somehow called to his mind the picture of a tree shorn of its
leaves. Since then, he had seen something new in her
each time.

She was still unapproachable until the afternoon

before she went for a holiday to her sister's, when she refused his offer to take her and the children there in his car—still the same obstinacy he had met in his office. But when he sat at tea with her and the two children and found how agreeable it was to share a simple meal, there was something about her that spread an air of comfort, and if he shut his eyes he could have imagined himself at home with his mother. Motherliness was the word for it. Why was he so drawn to her house—was it because of herself with her beauty, or was it just seeing her in her own house? There was wisdom in all she said tonight, speaking directly to the unconscious because of all that the years had taught her. Yes, he was disappointed, hoping she would do something towards taking what he had to offer her— the comfort that money brings, less work to do, while he enjoyed the pleasure of her company and her care of his house. He failed, however, to imagine her in his house: without the children, perhaps, but not with them. The children belonged to the other house with its half-worn chairs, chairs with their own history.

He knew at heart that he was not madly in love with her as he had been with Elizabeth, but he never expected that to happen again. Lora would bring him comfort for a while, at least. There might be problems with the children—he could not know how they might develop, but he knew by now that if she ventured to take a chance, she would keep a fair balance between him and the children. It might be that this was what restrained her, if only it were possible to read her mind. In spite of her explanations and her reasons, they all sprang from her intellect and not from her heart. She might still be in love with Iolo and that held her back. It sometimes happened that people were loved in spite of their failings, loved even more than those who came nearer being perfect, weakness calling for pity. If she had agreed to go away with him and give her husband grounds for divorce, would he, Aleth Meurig, have thought more of her? Was it not because she was unattainable that he craved for her? He could not answer his own questions. He switched off the fire and waited

175

for it to cool down. Then he drew the curtains and looked across towards Lora's house, wondering what was going through her mind. There was light in one window, sure to be Rhys's bedroom. Her mere presence in her house was company for him. But what if she left? He could not imagine her doing so. Unlike others who have been refused, he had no wish to go out of her sight—in itself a proof, if he needed it, that he was not head over heels in love with her. He dragged his way upstairs, hoping to be able to sleep, and to forget.

* * *

While Lora was at Bryn Terfyn, and Annie and Loti had made their own tea: salad, sardines and grated cheese was all it would run to in those days of scarcity. Loti washed up, then went back to the parlour where she found Annie staring at the fire in silence, chin on her left hand.

"What's the matter with you?" Loti asked.

"Just thinking," said Annie.

"You've done more thinking than talking since you came back from your holidays."

"I warned you when I came here that I might be difficult to live with."

"There's nothing difficult about living with someone who's dumb, except that it's strange when as a rule you're so talkative."

Annie did not reply.

"Would you like me to leave the house?"

"Do what you like, I don't care."

"Right. I'll look for somewhere else. I'm sure to find somewhere, though I don't want to go."

"Don't be silly—you know how hard it would be, and how lucky you are to be here."

"That's what I think, but I don't want to be a burden to you, and you were here first."

Annie turned her head and looked Loti in the face.

"Don't be so ridiculous—I'd be just the same as I am if you went as far as New Zealand. I'm just fed up with life generally."

"Are things as bad as that in school?"

"I doubt whether the school's to blame. I expect I'd be just the same if I were in your place."

"I wonder!"

"What do you mean?"

"You'd be working with men, not with women."

"That may be why you're so contented."

"Don't be so sniffy—you know perfectly well that men don't interest me any more."

"I'm sorry."

A long silence followed, and then Annie said she was going out.

"I don't think I'll come with you," Loti said. "I'd better keep an eye on the children till Mrs Ffennig comes back."

"I didn't ask you to come, did I?"

"No, but there was a time when you'd have been glad of my company."

"I think I'd better be alone tonight." She put on her hat and came to look in the mirror.

"Don't forget," she said. "You can be too much of a slave to people."

"There's no slavery in doing a bit of kindness like this—you don't appreciate the comfort you get here."

"I pay for it, don't I?"

"Yes, but very little. Pity you didn't have three months with Mrs Jones and pay as much as I did there, then you'd realise it."

"I don't know," said Annie. "This house has changed completely since Mr Ffennig went away."

"Were you in love with him?"

"Don't talk nonsense—you've no idea what the house was like then."

"Then it must be me who's put you against it."

"No, it's this perpetual coming and going." She went out and banged the door after her.

Loti sat and wondered. She had never seen Annie like this before. True, she was not quite herself that night in May when she came to tell of Iolo's disappearance, but nothing like tonight. Of course that event had brought about a complete change in the house:

until then all was quiet and seemed settled, Annie full of praise for her lodgings. As far as she could see, Annie was every bit as comfortable, except that she, Loti, was there. So it must be having to share the parlour that made her so bad-tempered and cantankerous. And yet, at times she was all right. She decided to tell her definitely she was going to look for somewhere else, and then she remembered that Annie was always happy when Aleth Meurig was one of the company. She had taken his side in the argument the previous night. How she gazed at him, her eyes shining! Was she in love with him? Or was it that she just wanted to get married to someone, no matter who? She was nearly twenty-nine, and had said she was sick of school. Tonight she thought Annie had been cruel, to her and to Mrs Ffennig behind her back. Perhaps she felt that while she was on holiday she had lost some degree of friendship with Mrs Ffennig, for they had both been very friendly. But Loti was determined to find new lodgings and to tell her so tonight. However, she began to feel sorry for Annie—and for herself. After all, Annie ought to be happy, having a good home to go to for the holidays, better salary (she did not have to mend her underclothes); while she herself was homeless, unless you could call her aunt's house, where she was just tolerated and said goodbye to cheerfully, a home.

And yet, she felt she could not leave Mrs Ffennig. Annie might be right in saying that the atmosphere in the house had changed. She heard Mrs Ffennig come in and dried her eyes in case she found signs of crying. She felt better now, and got down to work. After all, she did have an incentive.

Soon she heard the front door opening, Mr Meurig and Annie coming in, talking and laughing, a different Annie from the one who went out. When she came into the room, Loti took no notice and went on reading. Annie sat by the fire, glancing through some women's magazines. Mrs Ffennig came in with tea and biscuits on a tray, very red in the face. Loti thanked her, but Annie kept on reading. While they were drinking their tea, Loti said, "Look, Annie, I've decided to go and find somewhere else to live."

"Why?"

"I've told you why."

"And I've told you there's no need to."

"I feel responsible for bringing in all this unpleasantness. You used to have this room to yourself, no-one to disturb you, to be a weight on your mind."

"I've already told you that you're nothing of the sort. Don't you realise that if you go, Mrs Ffennig would find someone else to share the room with me, or ask me to go so that she could find two who'd get on together?"

"No, I didn't think of that."

"She must need the money, and it pays her better to have two—she'd still have to pay the same to the woman who comes in to clean if I was here on my own." Loti saw the point.

"But we can't go on like tonight for both our sakes. If you like, I'll go to the kitchen to Mrs Ffennig, except that I couldn't do much work there."

"There's no need for that. Perhaps it's I who ought to find somewhere else."

"Now it's you who's talking nonsense."

"Yes, I don't know what's the matter with me."

"Can't you tell me?"

"It isn't easy—I feel I ought to have a house of my own. I don't want to go on teaching, or I'd look for another school. That isn't what I want."

"Do you know what you want, or are you just one of those restless people who don't know, except that they're fed up with life as it is?"

"I know perfectly well what I want—I want to get married. I'm surprised to find I can admit it to you."

"There are no secrets between friends."

"Loti, I've behaved disgracefully towards you."

"I knew there was something wrong, but I thought you were going to be really ill."

"It may be an illness, but it's getting worse and not better."

179

"That's because you're unhappy at school."

"No it isn't," said Annie, as she began to cry. "I know quite well what it is. Jealousy, pure jealousy. There's Mrs Ffennig with a husband, and another man in love with her, while I'm free to marry and nobody cares for me."

"Forgive me for asking, but does Mr Meurig come into this?"

"I'm madly in love with him, but when he comes here, he has no eyes for anyone but Mrs Ffennig."

Loti ran her fingers through her hair, looking at Annie, utterly astonished.

"I don't know what's come over us all," she said. "We're like a lot of goldfish in a bowl, going round and round and never coming out."

"So we are," said Annie. "Perhaps Mr Ffennig has done the best thing by running away and doing what he wants."

"Yes, but that kind of happiness doesn't last. He'll soon be tired of it, and if I know anything about Mrs Amred, he'll tire of her quicker than anyone."

"Is anybody *ever* satisfied?"

"Yes, plenty. But once you start finding fault, good-bye to peace of mind."

Annie said nothing, but kept looking into the fire, while Loti did not know whether all this was matter for laughter or tears. Her friend was not very attractive to look at, except for her lily-white complexion, but then you would not tire of her quickly. Plump and short-necked, by the time she was fifty she would be what you could call a comfortable sort of body, hair still fair, face unlined. She would make a good wife for some man and keep him in comfort.

As she went to bed, Loti noticed that Annie did not come to say goodnight to Mrs Ffennig.

XXIII

"I don't want to go to hospital," said Rhys in bed next night while his mother was trying to argue with him.

"Don't you want to get better?"

"Yes, but I don't have to go to hospital for that—I can get better at home."

"Who's going to look after you?"

"I'll be all right while you're in school—it's not for long—and Mrs Jones will be here every day to give me a drink."

"That would be fine if your stomach was all right, but the doctors want to keep an eye on you every day."

"I'm not very ill."

"Of course not, but they want to find out what's wrong, and then they can cure you."

"They could do that here while I'm in bed."

"The doctor can't be here all the time just to keep an eye on you, and there's more than one doctor in the hospital. You see, Rhys, there might be a sore there, and if it bursts there'd be trouble and you'd be ill for the rest of your life and couldn't eat the things you like so much."

Rhys, thus cornered, played with the sleeve of his mother's jumper, turning it this way and that. His mother put him to lie down and wiped the sweat off his forehead. She felt guilty at letting the boy get into this state without noticing it. He must have suffered greatly to be so ill, while she bothered about her own troubles without thinking of that. He had become very thin.

"I'd go there willingly if you'd come with me."

"But I'm not ill."

"I meant if you came to look after me."

"Where would we get money to live on?" He thought for a while, and then said, "It's a pity things have gone this way, isn't it?"

"Yes, bach," she said as she ran her fingers through his hair. "But things will soon get better, and worrying won't bring it about any sooner. Think of Uncle Owen—he's made up his mind to get better."

"Yes, but he's allowed to stay at home."

"For a while, yes. He isn't suffering from what you are, and he may have to go to hospital, and they've very little money."

"Dafydd is lucky, isn't he? Healthy and plenty of money."

"Don't talk like that. Things may be different for him one day, while we're all right."

"You're not sure?"

"You can't be sure of anything. You try to go to sleep. The doctor says you want a lot."

"I'll do my best."

"That's the way to talk! I'll look in on my way to bed."

As she turned towards the door, he said, "Mam, if I go to hospital, will Dad get to know?"

"I've no idea."

"Aunt Esta could write to him, couldn't she?"

"She might."

"I don't want him to come to see me."

"I'm sure he won't."

"But you've just said you can't be sure of anything."

She was cornered for an instant. "It's easy to stop him coming if you don't want to see him."

"Will you promise?"

"Yes."

"You're not sure?"

"Yes I can, and I will."

"I don't want to see him because he's been so unkind to us, hurting us. Sometimes I feel I'd like to kill him."

"You mustn't think of such things, Rhys! It isn't right."

"What *he* did isn't right either."

"No, but hating him won't make us any happier."

"Don't *you* hate him?"

"Good gracious, no!"

"Do you still like him?"

"No, but I don't hate him."

"Why?"

"I can't explain it to a child like you." Nor to myself, either, she thought.

"I don't want to see him. Perhaps I'll stop hating him if I don't see him."

"Go to sleep now."

She went downstairs more disturbed in mind than when she went up.

She was surprised to find Aleth Meurig in the kitchen, for she had said goodbye to him last night.

"How's Rhys?" he asked.

"Rather poorly, I'm afraid." Her lower lip began to tremble. "The doctor doesn't think he's got an ulcer yet, but it might come—he says the boy's in a very nervous state, and that I can well believe."

"Has there been anything strange about him?"

"Yes, when I look back, though I didn't see it at the time. He's been hanging round me all the time, as if he was afraid of something happening to me, and now he's just said he'd like to kill his father."

"Heavens above! All this must have been brewing up inside him ever since his father left."

"He's very sensitive."

"Like his mother."

"No, like a child."

"Does he know anything about the money?"

"Not so far as I know."

"Is there anything I can do?"

"Yes, there is. I'm going to ask a favour of you, now, and it's to keep Iolo away from the hospital, if you can."

"You surely don't think he'll come to see the boy?"

"Not of his own choice, perhaps, but you never know what Esta will do. She may write and say he's on the point of death, or something like that. Or of course she might not."

"I'll do it willingly—it's a delicate business, and hard

183

to say whether it would be better to speak to Esta or telephone Iolo."

"Or write to him before Esta can."

"Yes, he might think things are worse than they are if I telephone. Does Miss Ffennig know Rhys is ill?"

"I don't think so."

"There's time to catch the post if I hurry."

"It's very kind of you."

He came back later, having written as tactfully as he could about the situation. He said the boy was not seriously ill, but on account of his nervous condition, a visit from him might do him harm. He did not really think it a sensible idea to write to Iolo, for if even he heard of the boy's illness he might not have had the slightest idea of visiting him. It would only give him occasion to jeer at his old employer and his wife just because they thought he cared. But of two evils, this was probably the least harmful. It gave Lora some peace of mind on one issue at least, though she too might have thought that Iolo would make light of it all. Still, it was ridding her of one of her many fears, although she had to demean herself in the process of making sure. She wanted no more trials for Rhys or for herself.

While Meurig was out, she wondered whether or not to talk to him about Derith, for he might hear from someone else.

"Tell me if I'm in your way," he said.

"Not at all. It's good to be able to talk, even if I don't talk very sensibly tonight. Have you heard about Derith?"

"Not a word." She told him about the thieving at school.

"I'm really sorry for you."

"It's had less effect on me than I expected. It's hard to explain, unless it's because I accepted her own explanation completely."

"Not knowing much about children, I can't say. But it does look like spite, seeing she didn't eat any of the things she stole. The danger lies here, that if she has a grudge against anyone, she'll do the same again. And if that keeps on happening, magistrates and the like wouldn't accept the explanation. Besides, people have a right to the safety of their possessions."

She did not reply, disappointed by his reaction. But then Derith was not his child.

I'm at it again. Every time I open this diary to write in it, something new has happened. The last time, it was Derith's stealing now it's Rhys's illness. It's simply overwhelming, and it's no use telling one's self that the darkest hour comes before the dawn. You could fall into the depths in the instant between dark and dawn. Having a child in hospital is no worse for me than for many others in the same position. I'm not afraid of what may happen to his body, but I am concerned about the effect on his mind. I can't forget his broken-hearted crying when they took him into the ambulance, his "Mam, I'm frightened" ... I can't get it out of my mind. I nearly gave way and insisted on their bringing him back to the house, but I must be firm. It may be that this separation, so cruel for him, so heart-rending for me, will cure him permanently.

I must harden myself more, and dismiss Iolo from my mind for ever. I can see now how wrong I was. I must leave this place. I wonder how much the children's playing the other night hurt Rhys. What was he frightened of? Death? The fear of death always haunted me when I was a child, and children are afraid to talk about it to anyone because no-one can give them comfort, for we are all ignorant about that untrodden country. Was he frightened of being away from me? I'm glad there's no danger now of Iolo coming back and making things worse. I had to sink my pride in asking a favour of Aleth. The lesser of two evils, but he could not understand. Naturally, as a solicitor, he was concerned about other people's property when talking about Derith. For him, it was a coldly impersonal matter. I don't know why I worry so little about it, nor why I can write all this with Rhys in hospital.

I don't know what has come over Miss Lloyd—she only just managed to ask how Rhys was, and she used

*to be so friendly and cheerful. Now she's like sour milk—
what is happening to us all? I wonder how Owen is—
still unable to sleep, still reading Williams Parry and
finding comfort "from someone in the pangs of the night-
watches". I've been thinking a lot about what he said
the other night, that he never looked through the window
now. Does that mean that he has given up hope and no
longer wants to look at what he loved? It was a strange
thing to say.*

*Derith doesn't seem to realise what is happening,
playing with other children and enjoying herself. All
to the good. No-one could tell what went through her
mind when the ambulance went off—she looked at it as
people do at a passing bus.*

XXIV

There was a long queue at the hospital, and in spite
of her haste and bustle Lora found herself at the end
of it, blaming herself for being so late in starting. Now
and Guto were coming for the weekend because Miss
Lloyd was going away at half-term. She had been put
out by Miss Lloyd's attitude when she asked her if she
minded the boys sleeping in her bedroom, or alterna-
tively, she and Derith could sleep there and the boys
go to the attic. Here, now, in the queue, she could not
remember exactly what had been said because she was
so upset. Miss Lloyd had hummed and hawed, her face
void of any expression. After a moment's silence she
said, "No, it makes no difference to me" (if those were
her actual words) in so indifferent and unwelcome a
tone of voice that Lora saw at once that she would have
liked to refuse. Her anger showed in her face for a

moment and she nearly told her to leave and find other lodgings, but then she thought it beneath her dignity, especially as she herself would soon be leaving the town.

"Never mind, Miss Lloyd," she said calmly, "I can manage perfectly well. Derith can have Rhys's bed and I'll sleep on the sofa in the front parlour."

"No need for you to do that," the teacher said, somewhat more kindly.

After that, Lora's mind had wandered and time had gone by, so that now she had lost some of the half-hour she would have had with Rhys. When she got to the door she was surprised to hear the attendant say there were two women in with Rhys and she must wait until their time was up. She was so disappointed that she did not even try to guess who they were, tapping her feet impatiently, but when the attendant learnt that she was the boy's mother he told her to go in and to ask one of the women to come out. She could hardly believe her eyes when she went into the ward. On one side of the bed, her mother-in-law and Esta sitting like a screen between the bed and that side of the ward, Rhys with his back towards them, lying stock still. She went up to him and found him with eyes closed and tears on his cheeks.

"Hullo, Rhys."

"Oh, Mam! I thought you weren't coming."

"I was kept busy and didn't get here by the time the doors opened. Are you feeling better?"

"Much better, until these two came."

Lora looked at her in-laws. The mother, plumper than she used to be, didn't raise her eyes. Esta sat there, ill at ease.

"Tell them to go away, Mam."

"I can't do that, Rhys, everybody has a right to come here."

"I don't want to see them."

"This is your fault, Lora," said her mother-in-law, raising her head slightly and looking at the back of Rhys's neck.

"Hospital isn't the place to discuss things like that," Lora replied. "But if you came to see me I could prove it isn't."

"You've kept the children from Iolo's family."

"Derith comes to see you whenever she likes, and I've never told Rhys to keep away."

Rhys turned towards his grandmother and aunt and began screaming, "Go away! Go away!"

Silence in the ward, everybody looking at them. Lora trying to calm the boy as he kept sobbing into his pillow. A nurse came to see what was happening, but the two women were on their way out by then.

"It's all right, nurse...he'll soon recover...just a family squabble."

"He's been much better recently, and beginning to enjoy himself, aren't you, Rhys?"

"Yes...I'm very sorry, nurse."

Lora began to feel queer, the world growing dark around her.

"Nurse, please could I have a drink of water?"

"Sit down, Mrs Ffennig."

The nurse was soon back to find Lora's head down on Rhys's bed, and Rhys's voice sounding far away.

"What's the matter, Mam?"

"There—feeling better, Mrs Ffennig?"

"Yes thank you, nurse."

"I'll call the doctor."

"There's no need now, but I *would* like a word with him before I go home."

"What was the matter, Mam?" Rhys asked after the nurse had gone.

"Nothing, just the shock at seeing your grandmother and Aunt Esta. It would be better for you and me to be like Derith and not let anything bother us."

She lifted her head and looked at Rhys—she could see him clearly now. He looked so much better that no-one would think he had made all that fuss a while ago.

"You haven't said what was the matter with you?"

"I think I fainted."

"Are you all right now?"

"I feel better."

188

"Are Guto and Now coming for the weekend?"

"Yes."

"I wish I was home."

"There wouldn't be room for us all. You mustn't talk of coming home until you're really well again."

"But I'm much better."

"And you like being here, don't you?"

"Yes," he answered shyly, glancing at his mother.

"You needn't be afraid of saying so."

"Why?"

"You've got to learn to like other places besides home."

"Why?"

"So that you can learn to live."

After a moment's silence, he said, "But I can't help liking being at home, can I?"

"No, but you must learn to like other places too."

"But we never get a chance of going to other places, do we?"

"No, not now, but we will some day."

She was about to tell him that he must learn to like other people, too, but refrained in case he got upset again. She felt vexed with him at the moment for making such a scene in the ward, and thought that the old-fashioned way of whipping such tantrums out of children was better than the modern way of humouring them. She decided not to go to see the doctor, and making an excuse of her fainting to go straight home she even hardened herself enough to say to Rhys, "I may not come here tomorrow night."

"Why?"

"I don't feel too well, and I may have a couple of days in bed before Guto and Now come."

"Do you feel really ill?"

"No, but I shall be if I don't rest. Goodbye now."

"Goodbye."

Rhys did not turn his head as she left, and all she saw of him was his back, and that made her wonder whether he was fretting, or trying to harden himself.

Loti came to the kitchen to ask after Rhys as soon as she entered the house, but when she saw Mrs Ffennig sitting still, her face the colour of putty, she stood at the door.

"Come in, Loti, I don't feel very well."

"What's the matter?"

"I had something like a fainting fit in the hospital. I was upset before going, and my mother-in-law and Esta were by his bed when I got in, and Rhys made a dreadful scene. But I mustn't talk about it."

"You go to bed, Mrs Ffennig. I'll see to Derith."

"I'm afraid I must, I just can't stand on my feet. I'm sorry to bother you, but could you bring me a hot water bottle and some hot lemon?"

"Of course, straight away."

Lora was glad to get to bed. When Loti brought up the hot lemon she took a sleeping tablet, and in that half-sleepy state she wanted to go on talking.

"I've reached the very bottom tonight, Loti, and it's a case of sink or swim."

"You won't sink, Mrs Ffennig."

"I've definitely decided to go to my uncle's to live. I feel stifled in this house."

"I'm sure any change would do you good. Wouldn't it be better to go to London to Mrs Ellis for half-term?"

"I promised my sister's children they could come here, and I can't disappoint them. It's our only chance between now and Christmas."

"You think too much about other people, Mrs Ffennig."

"I'll think less from now on, and it would do children like Rhys good to have less notice taken of them. My sister's children don't get enough."

"If Rhys has too much, it's because it's all in one place. He has nowhere to go except home and school."

"True enough. If he had grandparents, uncles and aunts, all scattered about he could go to them, but here he's fussed over by me all the time."

"It can't be helped. Things are like that."

"Poor children!"

"Never mind the children, go to sleep."

"I don't know what's come over Miss Lloyd—she used to be so nice." Her eyes were half-closed as she spoke, and before falling asleep she could see her mother-in-law leaving the hospital, a broken-hearted woman, and all mixed up with this vision was the conviction that her own future was linked with Loti's.

"Now, Derith, drink your milk and then to bed."

"Why are you putting me to bed?"

"Your mother's ill."

"Will she go to hospital?"

"No such luck—she can't stay in bed."

"I don't want to go to bed."

"I'm sure you don't. I wish your mother was as lucky as you are, going to bed and having someone to look after her all day."

"Guto and Now are coming here."

"Do you like them?"

"Gosh, yes!"

"Their father is ill, isn't he?"

"Is he very ill?"

"He's in bed."

"Is mother very ill?"

"I don't know—no I don't think she is."

"Is she going to die?"

"Of course not."

"Do you like Bryn Terfyn?"

"I don't know—I've never been there. Do you?"

"Gosh, yes!"

"Would you like to go there to live?"

"Yes, but there's no room."

"Do you like Ty Corniog?"

"Is that where the man with a moustache lives?"

"He may have one for all I know. Would you like to go there to live?"

"Yes, with mother, and with father instead of the man with a moustache."

Loti asked no more questions: this was the first time the child had spoken of her father in her hearing, and she wondered what was going through the child's mind.

"Can I see mother before I go to bed?"

"She's asleep now."

"Will she be asleep tomorrow?"

"No, I don't think so."

Derith went to bed willingly enough after drinking her milk. When Loti went back to the parlour, Annie was standing by the mirror getting ready to go out.

"What's the matter now?" Annie asked.

"Mrs Ffennig is quite ill."

She stopped powdering her nose and asked, "What happened?"

"I'm not quite sure. Something upset her before she went to the hospital, and when she got there old Mrs Ffennig and Esta were sitting by the bed, and Rhys all in a tantrum. She was half asleep when she tried to tell me, so I'm not quite sure what happened. It's been too much for her, and she has decided to go to her uncle's to live."

A shadow of a smile flitted over Annie's face, slowly vanishing into the corners of her mouth.

"Were you talking to Mrs Ffennig before she went out?" Loti asked.

"Yes, why?"

"I was only asking."

"You'd make a good detective. You want to know what upset her, don't you?"

"It would be interesting to know."

"I can't see any reason for being upset about what happened between us. She asked if I would mind if the children slept in my room over the weekend, and I said I didn't."

"That wasn't enough to upset anyone."

"Not so far as I know. But she said she could manage by sleeping on the sofa in the parlour and putting the children in Rhys's bed."

After Annie had gone out, Loti kept on wondering what could have upset Mrs Ffennig, and came to the conclusion that it was the way in which Annie had offered her bed that caused it, for Mrs Ffennig's answer stressed her independence of mind.

The next evening Loti went to the hospital to see Rhys. His face fell momentarily when he saw her, but by the time she reached his bedside, he had changed completely.

"Don't be alarmed at my coming. Your mother has gone to Ty Corniog."

"What for?"

"What do you think? She's decided to go there to live."

"Is she better?"

"Much better—she slept like a log last night, and was on top of the world this morning."

"When do we go?"

"I don't know. Don't count your chickens before they're hatched."

"So you aren't sure?"

"As sure as we're here."

"I hope we go soon."

"You may say so, but I don't—I don't know where I'll go then. It's so hard to find a good place, and I do like your mother."

A smile spread over Rhys's face and he looked her in the eye, as if the answer he was trying to solve lay there.

"Why don't you come with us?" he asked. "There's a bus to town every day from just near Ty Corniog."

"There wouldn't be any room there."

"There might be—there are four bedrooms, and Uncle Edward has been sleeping in the parlour for some time now, and the hall goes right through the house— like this, see?" He drew a plan on the bed with his finger. "And there's a big outhouse, plenty of room to keep things in. But there's no bathroom."

"That doesn't matter, we'll wash ourselves bit by bit."

Rhys burst out laughing. "Uncle Edward's a funny old man."

"That doesn't matter—we're all funny, anyway."

"Am I funny?"

"You behaved very strangely last night, your mother says, and it made her ill."

Rhys looked down, running his finger over the quilt, and then looked up at her, trying to defend himself.

"But I was cross because Grannie and Aunt Esta had

193

been so cruel to Mam, and I wanted to kill them when they came before she did."

"Feeling better today?"

"I'm sorry now, and I don't think I'll do it again."

"I should think not—you must remember your grandmother is getting old."

"Old people can be very unkind."

"Just like children can, Rhys."

"You see, Miss Owen, it had been boiling up inside me for a long time, almost choking me every time I saw Aunt Esta coming to us. I feel better now, just as I used to after being sick."

"It doesn't come back?"

"No. Was mother vexed with me?"

"I don't know, but it made her quite ill." Rhys stifled a sigh. "Now Rhys, just think of Ty Corniog and the two mountain ponies there, and different children." Rhys suddenly sat up and reached a book from the cupboard.

"Oh Miss Owen, do look . . ."

"Call me Loti."

"I'll call you Auntie Loti."

"No, I'm not an aunt to anyone."

"Look what came from my class this morning, this book."

"It's a really good one—it will last you a long time. Wasn't it kind of them!"

"I didn't expect anything, for I've only just gone there, and I don't know them very well."

"They really must be very kind boys."

"You see, Auntie Loti, I didn't expect anything because I've never been the same with other boys since father left. The Bryn Terfyn children are different, because they understand."

"Anyone with sense would understand. You don't need to worry any more. When we get to Ty Corniog— if I'm allowed to come—we'll work hard for our exams. We'll turn the outhouse into a study, and turn the world upside down." Rhys laughed again and said, "It will be grand there, won't it?"

194

"Yes, so hurry up and get better and forget all that's happened."

"Are you sure mother isn't ill, Loti?"

"I don't tell lies unless I'm cornered! You'll see your mother tomorrow night, and you'll be surprised."

On the way back, Loti thought a lot about the situation in her lodgings. Tonight she had seen a totally different Rhys—instead of that downcast boy hanging round the house, a youngster with plenty of pluck. She did not think his mother had been right in thinking that too much attention had been paid to him: too much of one kind, perhaps, and that not the right one. She had read a great deal about men leaving their wives and children, and about women leaving their husbands and family, but it had never occurred to her to wonder what the effect was. In their complete silence about their subsequent history, no-one had ever thought about the feelings of those who were left. It was always assumed that they recovered in time. She thought Rhys had really rid himself of something during his outburst when his grandmother and aunt came to the hospital. He looked much happier today. Perhaps an outburst of some kind might rid Mrs Ffennig of her disappointment, and that she would be the better for it. She was much too quiet and tolerant, and that may have made the boy imagine things. But she had no right to interfere in Mrs Ffennig's affairs.

She was very surprised when she reached the house to find Mrs Ffennig sitting by the fire, having turned back from the bus that would take her to Ty Corniog. No, she wasn't ill, she said, and gave no reason for turning back, but Loti guessed that it was due to her uncertainty about the wisdom of taking the fateful decision.

XXV

Guto and Now's visit was not a success. From the moment they crossed the threshold Lora missed the presence of Rhys. To keep children interested in class was easy, not so to entertain two children in the house without the help of a child old enough to take the lead. Derith and Now were too young to fend for themselves once they had finished looking through Derith's books. An hour was enough to exhaust what window-shopping had to offer, and the excitement of seeing Rhys in bed in hospital lasted only a few minutes. The playing field helped for a while on Saturday afternoon, but by night Lora had come to the end of her resources. She knew that little Now was homesick, and as bedtime approached he followed Guto everywhere, almost choking as he ate his supper. Luckily he soon wanted to go to sleep, and Guto had sense enough to see that it would be better if he went with him. Lora hoped that things would be better in the morning, and so he was as he ate his breadfast and got ready to go to chapel. When Lora asked him if he was going to say his verses after the sermon, he put his head down on the table, but looked relieved when she said he need not. But in the middle of the sermon the floodgates opened. Lora's mind was wandering to and from the sermon, forgetting about the children, when suddenly little Now burst into tears by her side, calling out, "I WANT TO GO HOME TO FATHER!" She took him on her knee and soon quietened him, but the remainder of the service seemed very long.

The boy looked miserable at dinner, everybody

trying to distract his attention, his brother making all sorts of promises to him. They got through the day somehow, reading, finding old pictures in the attic, telling stories, eating sweets and playing games. She took the children to the playing field next morning and decided to send them home after dinner. That would give her sister time to finish the washing. She would go to Ty Corniog and ask her neighbour Mrs Roberts to look after Derith.

How different Bryn Terfyn looked today compared with summer, all so sad-looking, the paths wet and muddy, the hens huddled in corners, cows waiting at the gate. Owen's bedroom without a fire, and cold for anyone sitting there. Owen was cheerful in spite of everything, saying he felt better and hoping to be up in a few weeks. Soon, she thought, the lamps would be lit and the curtains drawn, with a long night before him. The same tomorrow, and the next day. What sustained a sick man? Hope, perhaps. She remembered Owen saying he no longer looked towards the sea: was he hopeful, or was he merely hiding his feelings? Bryn Terfyn seemed so changed today. She and the children had come here sooner than expected, and the atmosphere was somehow unpleasant, one of disappointment. She felt her heart had gone stone cold. She thought of her own crowded house in town, full of movement, nowhere to rest. Then her mind turned to Ty Corniog, a house unrelated to her past, virginal almost, where she could start a new life and make a new home with Loti and the children. A small flicker of light came through. Owen must get better, and she must help to bring it about. She could do that from Ty Corniog. From that moment there was no turning back.

Little Now did not look much happier for being at home, and as she left he began to cry and say that he would miss her.

"He doesn't know what he wants," said Guto. She felt they were all in the same boat, except Owen, who knew exactly what he wanted most, and she walked towards the gate to the sound of Now's tears.

She walked along the cart track between Bryn Terfyn and Ty Corniog with more spirit than she had known for weeks. The sky above the sea was blue-black, clouds scattered untidily, the wind cold and piercing, blowing the dead leaves into corners. A healthy feeling as the wind blew through her clothes and carried the scent of peat. It was light enough for her to see the puddles in the marsh, like eyes on the surface of a stew. No sign of life in Ty Corniog, the five front windows shut, five blind eyes staring at the sea. As she passed the kitchen window along the path to the back door she could see her uncle in his overcoat, back towards her, staring at the fire in the twilight, the lamp unlit. When he heard her footsteps he half-turned his head to listen.

"Lora, is that you?" he cried, without turning his head.

"Nothing wrong with your hearing, anyway."

"Yes there is, but I'd recognise your footsteps anywhere. Look, lass, get us something to eat. I'm too weak to move. I got a tin of meat the other day—open it."

Lora noticed that the house was not so clean as it used to be. Her uncle got up and went to the corner for some wood and put it on the fire, which soon blazed up. Soon they were eating comfortably enough. Lora bid her time. She was not going to tell him straight out that she was coming there to live, in case he changed his mind.

"This food is really good," he said. "I don't know when I had such a good meal. Pity you can't come here to live."

"What would you say if I told you I was thinking of doing so?"

"I'd be delighted. To tell you the truth, I'd almost decided to leave here and go to an old people's home or the workhouse or somewhere. The woman doesn't come here to clean any more."

"And I've decided to leave my house—I can't live in it any longer."

"Why? Haven't you enough money to live on, or what?"

"It isn't that. I'm just sick of it. I feel stifled."

"You're very welcome to come here. There are four bedrooms for you. I've brought the small bed down to the parlour for myself."

"Is there any room for my furniture?"

"I can get rid of any things you don't want and sell them, and I'll put all I want to keep here in the kitchen and in my parlour where the bed is. The rest of the house is yours."

"If you like, I could put my furniture in the out-house."

"Why? I've no interest in anything in the house I don't use, and there's a man down in the town who gives a good price for old things."

"Why did you buy them to begin with?"

"Some of them were my mother's, and some I bought thinking I'd let the house to visitors in summer and live in the outhouse. But one lot came here and left without paying, the rogues."

"Do you mind if I go over the house again?"

"Go where you like."

Before she left, she and her uncle came to a perfect understanding, so perfect that Lora could hardly believe it would last. He did not want any rent, she could do what she liked in her part of the house, and Loti could come with her. She could have electricity put in, and she would look after him. She felt as light as a feather on her way back to the bus, longing to get on with her plans. Some day, it could be made into a four-roomed house. She tried to work out how much she would save by not having to pay rent—she realised that she would lose Miss Lloyd's money, and there were the bus fares. She would have to pay something to Aleth Meurig as well. But now she had something to aim at, and the will to achieve it was a great help.

She turned and looked at the hillside, lights shining sadly here and there. She knew she could not look forward to any pleasure in the community she would join in her new home—to do so would be to court disappointment. People were much the same everywhere, and these hillsides would never again be what they were to her in her childhood. Perhaps all that was only the romantic vision of a child. One of these lights came from Owen's bedroom: from here it was only one of many, and she could not identify it. Close at hand, it was a special kind of light, surrounded by illness and a sense of strangeness. Soon it would be the only light shining, distinguishing that house from its neighbours until dawn came and all were alike. She was angry that such trifles as a house and outhouse could occupy her mind for a moment, with all that suffering behind one of those small lights, and the suffering that of a man she loved like a brother.

She remembered that Linor's letter was still in her handbag—she had only glanced at it laying on the floor of the hall before starting out to Bryn Terfyn. She looked forward to reading it carefully by the fireside before going to bed. Its contents would surely confirm her opinion that going to re-start life in another place was the right thing to do.

Dear Lora,

I've never heard of anyone having so much trouble so suddenly. Comparing your quiet life some six months ago with that of today, I'm staggered to think that so great a change could come so soon. By running away, Iolo has opened the door for some strange beings to enter your house.

Don't worry too much about Derith: her explanation may be the right one. I heard of another such in school here, and when the child had a new teacher, it all came to an end. Children, especially the very young, can be very cunning.

Poor Rhys! I don't know what can cure him. It looks as if worry was the cause of his stomach trouble. He must get his father out of his mind first, and he must be liberated from you too. It's hard to say how to get a boy of his age to be more self-reliant. Do you think he wondered whether you were going to marry Aleth Meurig some day and that he saw himself losing you too? I believe that many children are five years older than their age, and perhaps what may help Rhys to stand on his own feet will be to see you living a life of freedom again, and alone. Did our grandparents have such problems?

I think you have been very wise in refusing to go off with Aleth Meurig. Don't misunderstand me: I'm not thinking about your reputation, but your comfort, and I think that is more important for you than anything else. I don't mean living in greater comfort—he could give you that—but your own peace of mind, your own life. He's probably a good man, but they don't always make the best husbands. Of course, it depends whom they marry. But by all accounts he's a very self-sufficient kind of man, and you'd be happier making life pleasant for a man who needs it more than he does. I'm sure he wants comfort, but not enough for you to drown him in it.

Some people are born to fill a gap in other people's lives, and I'm afraid there's not enough room in him for all the compassion that flows from you, and that you could not bear it from anyone else. Perhaps three years from now you will see more clearly where your happiness lies. I love you too much to think of your being once more disappointed. I like that Loti who is with you. I do hope your present troubles soon come to an end.

Ever yours
Linor

The letter gave Lora quite a shock, to think that what she wrote about had become history so soon. She did not worry much about Derith now, nor did her mind go back to Aleth Meurig, and even Rhys's health was less of an anxiety. To think that a few days ago she had asked a favour of Aleth Meurig, for Rhys's sake, even eager to do so then, for it filled her mind at the time. Tonight there was room for nothing but the move to Ty Corniog. Would life be always like this, must there always be something new happening before it became bearable? If so, the past meant nothing to her, although its influence would persist. What on earth could be that incentive Loti spoke about? True, Linor's letter had somehow grown old in the post between London and Aberentryd. But one thing remained: her friendly spirit and her understanding.

XXVI

The mists of autumn, and here I am in an empty house without table or chair, writing on the windowsill in the kitchen. How dreadful the house looks without furniture and pictures. It seemed all right as it was, but now it's only a skeleton. I was happy enough here, although it was only a superficial happiness. Writing this, I'm really happy, for I write with my eyes open. I now know why I wrote so much. I know that when I began, I was writing in despair so as to be able to survive, bowed down as I was. But even that changes its original purpose. At times I've used it to justify myself so far as Iolo is concerned, because my in-laws condemned me. I defended myself as if I was in a court of law, bearing all the guilt of the guilty. At other times I think I was trying to find the Iolo who disappeared out of sight and did not return, though I did think he would tire of Mrs Amred. So far as I am concerned, his great fault was to disappear, to turn his back on me, and to deceive me. As I try to find him, I feel he slips through my hands as quickly as the rat I saw in Bryn Terfyn cowhouse long ago, and that what stays in my mind is the colour of its tail and not the rat itself. But after trying and trying to understand him, and the relations between us, I think I've got to understand myself better, that in hard-

ening myself I've grown in stature, that inside me there is a spring, a force that will keep driving me on through life. I'll never come to the end of understanding Iolo or myself, though I've delved into the unseen and the unconscious. It's on the borders of these that dissatisfaction arises, and out of that comes this spring. Last night, when I was at Ty Corniog and finally decided to move there I felt the spring had run dry. And yet, it was in this mood of despair that I decided.

I know Owen had something to do with it. I myself had somehow ceased to exist, but Owen must get better, he simply has to. I know that peace of mind will never come again after what has happened. Until six months ago I was happy enough here. I was asleep then; now I have to be awake, and however much I may struggle, it will be with my eyes open.

A SELECTED LIST OF FINE NOVELS AVAILABLE FROM CORGI BOOKS

WHILE EVERY EFFORT IS MADE TO KEEP PRICES LOW, IT IS SOME-TIMES NECESSARY TO INCREASE PRICES AT SHORT NOTICE. CORGI BOOKS RESERVE THE RIGHT TO SHOW NEW RETAIL PRICES ON COVERS WHICH MAY DIFFER FROM THOSE PREVIOUSLY ADVERTISED IN THE TEXT OR ELSEWHERE.

THE PRICES SHOWN BELOW WERE CORRECT AT THE TIME OF GOING TO PRESS (MAY '86).

All these books are available at your book shop or newsagent, or can be ordered direct from the publisher. Just tick the titles you want and fill in the form below.

CORGI BOOKS, Cash Sales Department, P.O. Box 11, Falmouth, Cornwall.

Please send cheque or postal order, no currency.

Please allow cost of book(s) plus the following for postage and packing:

U.K. Customers—Allow 55p for the first book, 22p for the second book and 14p for each additional book ordered, to a maximum charge of £1.75.

B.F.P.O. and Eire—Allow 55p for the first book, 22p for the second book plus 14p per copy for the next seven books, thereafter 8p per book.

Overseas Customers—Allow £1.00 for the first book and 25p per copy for each additional book.

NAME (Block Letters) ....

ADDRESS ....

....